A regular columnist for Darling Magazine, Nicola Murray is a branding and an interpersonal impact specialist, conducting numerous seminars on a range of interpersonal impact and branding related topics for multinational companies. She is a member of the Society of Authors and bilingual in English and German.

A Certified Master Coach through the International Coaching Council (ICC) and Affiliate member of the Federation of Image Professionals International, Nicola has a passion for people and their potential.

Based on a true story, *Not What I Had in Mind* is an open hearted recount of a mother's burning desire to conceive and the trials, tribulations and comical moments experienced when this process doesn't take its natural course.

Nicola lives with her husband and two children in London.

Not What I Had In Mind

Nicola Murray

Not What I Had In Mind

Pegasus

PEGASUS PAPERBACK

A CIP catalogue record for this title is
available from the British Library

ISBN- 978 1 903490 51 8

*Pegasus is an imprint of
Pegasus Elliot Mackenzie Publishers Ltd.*
www.pegasuspublishers.com

First Published in 2005
Reprinted in 2011

**Pegasus
Sheraton House Castle Park
Cambridge CB3 0AX England**

Printed & Bound in Great Britain

Dedication

Written in loving memory of my beloved great aunt,

'The Duchess'.

I dedicate *Not What I Had in Mind* to Patrick and Grace, my
sweet angels, who've taught me that life is discovered in the
here and now and it is these quintessential moments which
crystallise into the memories of our yesterdays and the hopes
of our tomorrows.

Acknowledgements

There are a great many people I'd like to acknowledge who have in their own unique way been instrumental in the creation of this, my first book.

First and foremost, my husband, for his unconditional love and patience without you this book wouldn't have been possible.

I will forever be indebted to Dr Peter Beale, the surgeon who 'gave me my son'. You were Patrick's knight in shining armour at a time when I thought there wasn't a hope left.

To Dr Melanie Davies whose expertise made the miracle of conception a reality for me.

For my parents who thought they'd be free of the bondage of parenting once I'd left home, only to discover that grand-parenting would be the beginning of another era that would require a much deeper and more intense commitment to my life and its journey.

To Susan, my nanny, who walked the floors, the passageways and eventually, the walls to nourish my son, thank you.

To Anna Nkosi for the role you played, not only as my maternity nurse but also my confidant.

And last but most certainly not least to my beloved friend, Brett Belinsky, for his editorial genius, which has helped make this book exceptional in my eyes.

PART ONE

Chapter One

The sign read 'Accident and Emergencies'. That was us, in fact it just about summed up my state of mind quite accurately. As Benjamin and I pushed through the glass doors into the reception area the lady behind the desk asked us, somewhat dismissively, "What's the matter?" With that the tears I had fought to hold back until now, just flooded in.

How could anyone be so offhand when it came to matters of such urgency? I barely managed to communicate that my baby boy of four months had not eaten for twenty-four hours before the second torrent of tears began. Hopeless, just hopeless, after months and months of pent-up frustration and concern I had finally reached breaking point.

I did not care to fill her in on the history of William's eating problems, problems that had consumed my every waking hour, hours which of late had replaced sleep, since he was brought home from St Mary's Hospital along with his twin sister, Jessica.

"Oh Benjamin, when will this nightmare end, I can't take much more?" was all I could say as we waited to see our paediatrician. "It's not supposed to be like this!"

"If you don't pull yourself towards yourself Emma, I'm going to admit you!" Benjamin retorted and looked at me as if he no longer had any confidence in me. Emma Hogan, the one who was always in control and had everything in hand, was falling apart.

I never knew and still to this day don't know the exact reasons behind my difficulties in falling pregnant. Could it have been an eating disorder at the impressionable age of nineteen which only truly ended five years later; could it have been that I had polycystic ovaries and endometriosis, a condition which affects over two million women in the UK; could it have been that I simply had left having babies so late in life or did it boil down to pure genetics? Who knows and quite frankly there was nothing at this point I could do about any of the possible reasons so there was no real use in deliberating them any further.

My gynaecologist in South Africa had told me, however, after the laparoscopy, that my chances of falling pregnant were around sixty-five percent within two years and that during any normal cycle women only had a twenty percent chance of falling pregnant. Phew! If I thought about it in context of a relay race, I had been penalised, my feet had been tied and I was starting a lap behind my counterparts.

So today I decided to stop playing victim and to do something about it.

Benjamin and I had been trying to fall pregnant for over a year – nothing was happening, except of course a huge dose of great sex and tears enough to fill the Zambezi River as month after month the home pregnancy tests read negative. I had begun to wonder if these damn things actually worked.

I started off by searching my memory of friends that I could recall who had confided in me at some point about their difficulties in conceiving and decided to call Phoebe Carlyle.

Now Phoebe, being most definitely one of my admired friends, always immaculately dressed, well organised and on the surface certainly appeared fully au fait with everything, had given birth to twins two years earlier and had consulted the expertise of a fertility doctor in London.

Right, I thought, I'll call Phoebe, I had nothing to lose; pride seemed a luxury I could not afford to worry about. I had known Phoebe since I was a teenager, we had played hockey together and I felt comfortable calling her and confiding in her.

"Hi Phoebe, I wanted to confirm plans for Thursday next week and to ask you about the fertility doctor you consulted in London," I said as she answered the phone in as casual a voice as I could manage, trying to hold back the tears.

"Hi Emma, just about to call you myself. I've already made a reservation for six at Mano's on Preston, hope that's good for you? I've heard they play great jazz music. How can I help with the fertility stuff?"

With that I burst into tears, unwillingly letting go of any form of self-control. As hard as I tried this subject was too emotional to remain calm. I never could fathom how I remained so in control at work under the most challenging and emotive situations, while I broke down at the first mention of babies and fertility.

I finally stopped crying, took three deep breaths and continued the conversation. Phoebe had not said a word; she just waited patiently for me to compose myself.

"Well, Benjamin and I have been trying now for over a year and other than loads of sex, we've had no joy," I explained very openly, again trying to make light of a very emotional topic.

"Emma, I've been there and I know how you are feeling, believe me you're not alone so don't despair. I can recommend the consultant obstetrician and gynaecologist I used with utmost confidence. Her name is Dr Collins and she works out of one of the best Assisted Conception Units in London. They have one of the highest success rates in the UK and their research budget, mostly from donations, is one of the largest because of this. I'll e-mail you her contact details. The unit is based in the Private Patients wing of University College Hospital. It's dead easy to get there, only about a two-minute walk from the Warren Street tube station on the Victoria or Northern lines. Let me know how things go and Emma, I am at the other end of the phone if ever you want to talk about this."

"Thanks, much appreciated, I can't begin to tell you how much your support means. We'll see you and Stan next week," with that I replaced the receiver and sighed with relief. I secretly envied Phoebe and her ability to stay on top of things.

Perhaps I wasn't a freak of nature after all!

"Good morning," I said, as I spoke to the receptionist at the Assisted Conception unit at University College Hospital, "I would like to make an appointment with Dr Collins please."

"Let's see, you know she's extremely busy, the first available appointment is in three months' time I'm afraid. May I take your name and contact details?"

My heart fell, three months, I thought. Now that I've made my mind up to see someone how can I possibly wait that long!

"Is it possible to get an earlier appointment, I was referred to her by a friend of mine, Phoebe Carlyle?"

"Oh, in that case let me check again." That old adage, it's not what you know but who.

"Mmm.... yes, I have a slot available in three weeks' time, the 27th May at four. Can you make that?"

"Yes, thank you very much."

I felt a deep sense of relief but at the same time apprehensive. I had absolutely no idea what I was in for and it scared me.

When Benjamin arrived home that evening I poured him a beer shandy and told him about the appointment. We had spoken about fertility treatment on the odd occasion, but like most men, Benjamin preferred to hear only the key points not interested in the detail. His initial reaction was typical.

"Are you sure you aren't overreacting, we've only been at it for a couple of months?"

"No, it's been a year actually and I know for certain there's a problem and I know it lies with me. I'll need your full support if we begin a fertility programme; I hear it's not a pleasant experience."

"Relax! Why don't you go to your appointment, listen to everything Dr Collins has to say and then we can talk about it from there and decide once we know what it involves?"

"What questions do you want answered then, to satisfy your mind?" I pressed on.

"Ask what it costs, what the demands on your time especially with your work commitments will be and what's the chance of success?"

The conversation left me feeling hard done by. Benjamin damn you, it's not just me it's us!

I spoke only to one other person about my plans; it wasn't my mother, or a girlfriend as one might have imagined, but rather my Great Aunt Viv.

Viv and I had been close since I was young. When my mother couldn't watch me play hockey or collect me from school or take me to a party, Aunt Viv would always step in. If my parents went away, Aunt Viv would come and stay. If I was unwell or my brothers for that matter, Aunt Viv would spend hours at our bedside comforting us, keeping us occupied. Unlike most relationships in a family, ours had always been open and honest. I felt completely at ease confiding in her my deepest, most personal feelings and she never gave me away or betrayed that trust between us. Now that Benjamin and I had moved to the UK, it had become difficult to talk as frequently as we used to.

Despite this geographical distance, however, I continued to try and let her in on everything happening in my life as often as I could.

"Viv, it's Emma," I said.

"Hi darling, Emma-Beez. So good to hear your voice." Aunt Viv always called me Emma-Beez.

"Thought you'd like to hear my news. I can't seem to fall pregnant so I'm seeking help from a 'quack'," I said.

"Oh darling, did I not tell you during all those talks together that it doesn't always happen instantly?" Aunt Viv asked reflecting back.

"Oh, you made that crystal clear Viv, don't you remember that hockey coach boyfriend of mine. That was around the time you took me aside and explained the birds and the bees as one adult to another?" I remembered the occasion as if it was yesterday.

"Are you and Benjamin having enough sex then?" she laughed.

"We sure are, it's a little more complicated than that," I said.

"Emma, life's as complicated as you make it. In my book, keep things simple and you avoid the pimples." I laughed; she always made me laugh even during the most tense of moments.

"Are you keeping fit, walking a little?" I asked knowing that since her fall she had become more nervous and went out less and less.

"Yes of course. I can't give you reason to get angry with me now can I," Aunt Viv said, but not convincingly enough.

"No, you'll never catch a handsome man if you don't get moving," I said jokingly.

Aunt Viv was a spinster even though she had had many proposals throughout her life; I suppose it was circumstances that eventually prevented her from marrying. Two of her fiancés had been killed in the Second World War and she had never really recovered after the death of dear beloved Bobby, the man of her dreams. For years Mum and my Nan had arranged small jobs for her to keep her mind active and the income rolling in, but for whatever reason, and Viv had many, she would never take up the jobs. Happy to help take care of us, I never questioned her decisions until later.

Three weeks on I left work early to get to Warren Street, my mind racing now, as I had had little time since Benjamin and I first touched on the subject to think about it in more depth. Work had been hectic and in fact, I believe now, I had used work to help bury the subject for a while. I hated the thought of not being able to accomplish something I wanted. I felt defeated.

As I walked into the reception area past two other couples holding hands in the waiting room deep in conversation, thoughts rushed through my head: "I'm not like them, there's nothing wrong with me, just a little hic-cup nothing I few Clomifene tablets can't fix." I look back now and reflect on how embarrassingly naïve I was to think that in some way I was superior to these couples and that to have difficulties in falling pregnant meant you were inadequate, a failure.

"I'm Emma Hogan, here to see Dr Collins," I said quietly, worried someone might overhear my name. God forbid!

"Oh, yes, we have all your details on the computer, please take a seat, she won't be long."

I had had to send the results of my laparoscopy and Benjamin's semen analysis ahead of time, so imagined she was referring to these.

I tried to envisage Dr Collins and pictured her as being a woman in her late forties, wearing glasses, somewhat nerdish looking and rather aloof but professional. I imagined her as a female version of the head character in *Crime Scene Investigation.*

I did not have to wait to see if the image I had in my mind was accurate. There on the wall to my left hung a photograph of Dr Collins along with pictures of the other consultant gynaecologists and each member of staff in the unit. I was right about most things, but she had a very worldly look about her and green eyes that communicated sincere compassion.

"Hello, Mrs Hogan?" I heard a voice say, which took me by surprise

"Yes, that's me. You must be Dr Collins." Stupid comment, I thought. I followed her into her office and took a seat. I felt unusually calm and collected.

"Mrs Hogan, I believe you were referred to me by Mrs Carlyle, how are her twins? I have a picture here which must have been taken at eight weeks." And she pulled out a photograph Phoebe had sent her.

"They're fine, gorgeous children. Phoebe asked me to send her regards." I felt immediately at ease in her presence.

"Thank you, well what can I do for you?" she asked, and with that I began to lose my composure despite the numerous times I had rehearsed what I was going to say on the tube coming over. I was at a loss for words; I couldn't string the sentences together.

I asked for a moment while I gathered myself and began afresh, at which point Dr Collins lent over her desk and handed me a tissue from the tissue box in front of her. She's seen this all before I thought.

"My husband and I have been trying to conceive for over a year now and we've had no luck thus far. We would desperately like a child; my husband and I are getting older so feel we need to seek outside help. I had a laparoscopy six months ago due to pain in my pelvic area and abnormal periods, which is when they diagnosed endometriosis and polycystic ovaries. Phoebe recommended you to me, so I thought I'd make an appointment and seek your advice."

"When was your last period?" Dr Collins asked.

"I can't really remember it was so long ago. I was on the pill for eight years and always regular. I've been off the pill for a year and a half now and since my cycle is unpredictable. Sometimes I'll go for a month without a period!"

"Your laparoscopy shows that you have mild endometriosis and polycystic ovaries as you so rightly said. Both conditions would naturally hinder your fertility. Your husband's semen analysis results are good. He has a good count of healthy semen." As she said this I chuckled to myself thinking at least Benjamin has 'swimmers' and loads of them! I began to think about the film *Look Who's Talking*.

"Are you wanting children now or can you wait a few more months and continue trying unaided?" she was saying as I drifted back to the conversation at hand. I was not sure what had come over me of late; I seemed so easily distracted. Perhaps I was in denial, fudging the real issues to avoid revealing how depressed I really was not being able, like many of my friends, to effortlessly fall pregnant?

"Benjamin and I are ready to have children. We'd like to start sooner rather than later. I don't want to waste another year," I said decisively

"If you both feel that strongly then, I'll try not to get too technical in my explanation of what your general treatment options are. Feel free to ask questions. The first option is a course of Clomifene tablets taken orally to stimulate ovulation. Although this is the least invasive route and easiest to administer, I hasten to add that it's not generally recommended in cases where polycystic ovaries are present. The Clomifene tablets just tend to increase the number of ovarian cysts.

"The second option, would be to induce ovulation using gonadotrophins, FSH and LH, self-administered daily by injection. We then monitor the growth of the follicles via scans until they grow to full size, around 18mm-22mm. At this point we inject you with a substance called Human Chorionic Gonadotrophin (HCG) to bring on ovulation. We then advise you to have intercourse at predetermined times for the next few days when you are most fertile. That's the part most husbands find difficult, sex in their minds is supposed to be spontaneous. There is a twenty percent chance of success each cycle. I must warn you there's also a twenty to twenty five percent chance of twins due to over stimulation of the ovaries. That's why, as a precaution, we gradually increase the amount of gonadotrophins and at times you may get impatient with us.

"The last option and the most invasive is in vitro fertilisation (IVF). Basically the process is identical to the second option but once the eggs are released they are removed from the ovary thirty six to forty hours later. The eggs are fertilised with your husband's sperm in our laboratory and returned to the womb. You have a twenty to thirty percent chance of success, on average, each cycle. There are other options, but these are the most common."

As she spoke my head began to spin and I felt woozy. This was like a biology lesson. What am I getting myself into? I would be handing over custody, for a time, my most private functions to complete strangers, what an invasion of privacy! Where was the romance and surprise, wasn't falling pregnant supposed to be the most natural thing in the world? Clearly, with Benjamin and I it was going to be clinical. I thought of all the lists I always made for groceries and 'things to do'. I would just have to add one more action item: 'have sex with Benjamin tonight!' If my mother only knew, I thought to myself.

Now, Mum is a perfectionist as well as a devoted parent, which makes for a very powerful combination of characteristics! She tends to see the world through her eyes and to judge accordingly. Her children are perfect and no one can persuade her otherwise. How was she going to handle the news that I was devoid of the natural ability to fall pregnant, a stigma only 'other' lesser mortals suffered from? I decided not to tell her, at least not for now anyway, one less stress factor to manage. I knew only too well that the news of my fertility treatment would spread like wildfire if I did, and would become the subject of many dinner parties, bridge lessons and ladies' teas. I could already hear the babble of conversations in my head: "What, your daughter is having IVF?" a friend of hers would say. "I'm sure it is linked to her eating disorder at nineteen. I kept telling her and I warned her, do you think she listened then, well perhaps she'll listen now but it may be too late," my mother, proud of her foresight back then, would say, and inadvertently embarrass me behind my back. And sometime along the line, I'd receive a telephone call from one of Mum's friends asking me how the fertility treatment was going and informing me that I was the subject of a prayer meeting.

An hour passed in Dr Collins' office and I left the hospital with a sense of bewilderment and self-doubt. I wasn't sure I could handle this.

Meanwhile Benjamin was travelling every third week for business and I too had been to India, Australia, Singapore and the USA for work. This travel itinerary spelled disaster as the backdrop for trying to fall pregnant. Each treatment cycle had a few days within which I had the best chances of falling pregnant and Ben needed to be around on those days and nights.

"Benjamin, we need to cut back on our travels for a while." I broached the subject tentatively one evening a week later over dinner. "We have to be in the same city let alone the same bed to conceive. Can you stay put for the next three months while we give the fertility treatment a go?" I knew how hard it would be for Benjamin since the nature of his work necessitated travel.

"I'm due to travel to South Africa next month for a week. There's a big deal we're involved with there," he said, and then seeing the tears begin to trickle down my cheekbone, he hastily added: "Can't we start the fertility treatment the week I get back? I'll make sure that I am in town for a couple of months, promise."

"As long as you keep your promise. Remember I said you had to be in or out from the start, you can't sit on the fence darling. I have made an appointment for four weeks' time." I was already nagging and we hadn't even begun treatment yet. I gave him the date and he wrote it down in his palm pilot.

"Besides, all I need is your semen!" I said jokingly, but I underestimated how much more of Benjamin I'd need as the programme progressed.

Chapter Two

The weeks passed and I kept noticing how many pregnant woman there were in the streets of London and by looking at the size of their stomachs guessing how far along they were, something I never really studied before. It was becoming an obsession. My dreams even took on a new focus.

My first appointment with Dr Collins was on Wednesday and as luck would have it, a videoconference with our Washington office had been scheduled to take place at the same time. Dr Collins had warned me during our first appointment that the demands on my time would become increasingly challenging as we progressed with the programme and that work might conflict with the predetermined fertility schedule. At the time I hadn't paid much attention to her warning, assuming as I always did, that it would all work out somehow and I would be able to cope despite my long working hours. The fertility treatment would simply work around my existing life not visa versa.

Was I in for a shock! It never occurred to me to take into account the emotional strain and how this would affect my concentration at work. Instead of being focused on new market opportunities and clients I became increasingly pre-occupied with the thought of having a child.

Still, I had no idea if the treatment would work and to run the risk of telling my boss, which might jeopardise my seniority status in the firm, was, I foolishly believed at the time, too high a price to pay.

I was running late since I had managed to reschedule the video conference for an hour earlier, but as always it ran over none-the-less.

Having already sprinted all the way down Holborn Viaduct to the nearest underground I found myself fighting against time. I was never going to make it to Warren Street in fifteen minutes; all I needed now was for the Central or Victoria lines to be down. Today must have been my lucky day; both lines were running and on time.

I arrived at University College Hospital out of breath with sweaty underarms, feeling rather dishevelled and bursting for the toilet. I ran straight past the receptionist who was in the process of asking, "May I…." I never heard the rest as I headed directly for the toilet.

Much relieved, feeling more human again, I approached the reception desk.

"I gathered you were in need of the toilet," the polite receptionist volunteered.

'Yes, nothing like the London underground to remind you of what it feels like to run a marathon!" I said tongue in cheek. "I'm Emma Hogan, here to see Dr Collins."

"Dr Collins is expecting you, please follow Lucy one of our gynaecologists." My hands were clammy and I had a slight headache. She took me into a room I had not seen before and asked me to take my clothes off from the waist down and to then stretch out on the examination bed and cover myself with the clean white sheet she then handed to me.

"Is this your first encounter with fertility treatment?" Lucy asked as I undressed behind a curtain

"Yes, I'm not sure what to expect and I'm generally an impatient person."

"Well, I'm one of the gynaecologists here, you'll be seeing a lot more of me over the next while. Patience here is a virtue and one I'd learn to acquire if I were you. I wish you all the success. I will be doing an initial internal vaginal scan to see what your ovaries look like today before we start with the gonatrophins. Dr Collins will be in shortly to analyse the scan results and make a decision from there."

Oh goodness, I suddenly remembered, I forgot to wax my legs!

This was certainly not the first time I had felt naked, exposed and vulnerable while being prodded about down there in a medical sense. Something we woman endure each time we go for our regular check-ups! Little did I know that this was the beginning of many probes. I would eventually become numbed to taking my clothes off and being examined by doctors. Any shyness about carrying a few extra pounds, hidden blemishes or not having waxed for two weeks would soon disappear as those concerns paled to insignificance in relation to the concerns I was going to have moving forward.

"As you can clearly see, there are a few small cysts on your ovaries consistent with polycystic ovarian syndrome," Lucy was saying as Dr Collins tapped on the door and walked into the room.

"Hello Mrs Hogan, how are you feeling about starting treatment?" Dr Collins asked warmly.

"A little apprehensive but excited. I'm hoping that my body responds to the treatment," I said.

"I am hopeful of a positive outcome too, but it may take time and it may require more than one cycle of treatment, so you'll have to be patient and committed. Now, let's take a closer look at your ovaries before we begin with a small dose of gonatrophins to help stimulate egg growth and then ovulation." Dr Collins remained professional at all times.

"Mmm, there are a few cysts on the ovaries, but not as many as I'd thought there'd be. That's good news. I'll start you off on a very small dose of FHS and LH, since we'd rather go slowly even if it means it takes a week or so longer to grow the follicles to a mature size, than give you too high a dose to start. There's always a possibility as you know, of a multiple pregnancy with any form of fertility treatment." Dr Collins always seemed to make a concerted effort to be as frank as possible, something I appreciated.

"Would you like one of the nursing sisters, Kim, to administer the first injection today or are you comfortable to do the first one yourself at home tonight?"

All of a sudden I felt queasy, being the sort of person that simply has to smell a hospital to faint let alone fiddle with injections!

"No, no I would really like Kim to do the first injection. I hate having blood taken so I'm not sure how I'm going to handle injecting myself every day," I said honestly.

"Well, if you would prefer we could inject you here every day at the hospital but I'm not sure with your work schedule if that's practical. Either way, chat to Kim about it." Dr Collins left the room along with Lucy. Kim and I were left to sort out the logistics.

Once dressed, Kim took me through to another room. I noticed that the rooms were all decorated in a way that gave them a friendlier feel than clinical wards in a hospital.

"If you'll jump up onto that bed over there I need to take a swab to make sure that everything is OK, it won't take a minute. You're familiar I'm sure with pap smears?" I nodded.

"Well, this will feel very much the same as those," Kim said, trying her best to make it sound all so easy. No one ever tells you what a pap smear really feels like – like a baseball bat with pincers is being shoved up your vagina!

"Right, I now need to take some bloods to test for rubella, to make sure you're not pregnant and to test your thyroid function. These we do as a matter of course for all our patients." As she took the blood I looked away, feeling light-headed I asked for a drink of cold water.

"You can jump down now and I'll show you how to administer the injections. You can then decide if you want to come to the hospital every day or if you can manage on you own at home," she said, as she lent over and picked up a long gadget.

"I'll use this contraption here, a plunger, which will make it even easier for you." Kim pointed towards something that resembled those springs one used as a kid to store sweets in. I was obviously not the first to fear needles otherwise why on earth would anyone have invented this seemingly trivial object.

As Kim demonstrated I began to understand more fully what type of commitment this required and how focused I would need to be, it was bad enough remembering to take the pill everyday!

Looking back, what a complete waste of time! I wouldn't have fallen pregnant anyway.

"You need to administer the injection at approximately the same time each day. Make sure you get rid of all the air bubbles before placing the syringe into the plunger here. Find the fattest part of your thigh, with you this may be difficult as there isn't much fat on you! Dab the area with the antiseptic lotion using a piece of cotton wool and place the plunger just above the surface of the skin. When you're ready, depress the plunger and voila it's over." Kim was really trying to make this easier for me. I could empathise with diabetics who did this everyday of their lives as a matter of survival.

"Will there be any swelling after the injection?" I asked, vanity being my first concern. Since moving to London from South Africa six months earlier, my once gorgeously tanned legs were now transparent, any little blemish stood out like a blonde in the streets of a small Italian village.

"No, there shouldn't be. I advise that you try to inject yourself in a different place on your thigh each time. That way it'll help prevent bruising." Kim handed over to me a small blue bag. "Here's your 'bag of goodies,' inside you'll find all the syringes, cotton wool buds, bandages and a plunger. I've given you enough supply of Menopur to last you until your next visit in two days' time."

This little inconspicuous bag was to become my trusted companion. Mum, was coming to visit us from South Africa for four nights on route to visit my older brother. I had to hide this bag somewhere where she wouldn't discover it, I thought to myself.

My mother never missed a thing. But where in our shoebox of a one-bedroom apartment would I find a secret hiding spot?

Of course, the one place no visitor would look, even she wouldn't have the audacity to check there; Benjamin's underwear drawer.

"Thank you, Kim, wish me luck," I said, as I made light of the task ahead of me.

"We're all holding thumbs, this is just the beginning, pace yourself a little Emma. See you Friday."

Arriving back at the apartment, Benjamin was working late that night. I decided to go running in Kensington Gardens, a pastime Benjamin and I often did together if we weren't at the gym or working late. Being May, London was beginning to come into full bloom. Our street, Brunswick Gardens, was one of the prettiest streets in Kensington. In springtime, the cherry blossoms were spectacular, creating an avenue of what seemed like clouds of pink tinted snowflakes stretching upwards and outwards to infinity.

The park was bustling with people, some walking their dogs or sitting on benches or on the lawns, other more energetic types rollerblading or jogging. As I ran along the many footpaths through Kensington Gardens and into Hyde Park I felt elated, full of hope that perhaps I might actually be able to conceive and bare Benjamin's child after all!

I decided to call Aunt Viv – I needed a woman to talk to. I didn't think about the costs from a mobile phone, that hadn't entered my mind. I dialled her number hoping she'd be at home.

"I've begun fertility treatment," I said after a while.

"You've what?" Aunt Viv sounded confused.

"You know, needles and things to help me fall pregnant," I said.

"What on earth are you doing that for Emma-Beez?" Viv sounded shocked.

"I thought you'd support me not question my motives Viv." I was disappointed.

"Now, now Emma-Beez, don't get all upset. I'm just cautioning you not to rush headlong into motherhood. It's harder than you imagine," were Aunt Viv's words of wisdom.

"Well, I'd believe you if you had had nine children, but I'll reserve comment at this time seeing you've had none my darling," I said tongue in cheek.

"You are still as cheeky as ever I see," she said.

"I'll keep you posted and call often to let you know how it's going,' I promised.

"How what's going?" Viv asked, and to my surprise I realised perhaps in the year I'd not seen her that she'd aged.

"Tell me how Benjamin is." Aunt Viv changed subjects without knowing she really had.

"Fine, why do you ask?" I said.

"Remember him. He's still your priority you know," Aunt Viv said, as we ended the call and I promised to let her know how the injections were going. As I put my mobile back into my pocket it dawned on me that my Great Aunt Viv, now eighty-seven, who'd always been there for me, might be growing old.

A little unnerved by the conversation I had had with my aunt, I took my time in walking home. By the time I returned home, Benjamin had already started cooking supper.

"There you are. Tried phoning you on your mobile and realised when it rang in our bedroom that you were either at the gym or in the park. I started dinner."

"Hi sweetheart, I'm sorry, I was enjoying being out so much that I forgot all about the time. How was your day at work?"

"Oh, not bad. More interesting though, how did your appointment with Dr Collins go today, I've been thinking about you all day?" Benjamin had obviously also been thinking about the prospects of having a child as much as I.

"Great, only thing though," I paused as I walked through to the bedroom to fetch the little blue bag, "I have to stab myself every day for the next while." I handed him the bag to look inside. "And you're going to have to hold my hand, you know how I hate anything to do with needles."

"What's the bag for?"

"Just take a look inside," I said.

"You didn't tell me you'd have to become an addict," Benjamin said jokingly. "It all looks mighty complicated to me. Have you already given yourself one today?" he asked.

"No, I chickened out, the hospital kindly did the first one thank goodness. I thought I'd keep the bag of goodies in your underwear drawer. Mum is coming to stay on the weekend and the last thing I need is for her to discover the bag."

"Sure, that's fine, is there any room left for my underwear!" Benjamin said, more as a rhetorical remark than a true question. "Remind me how long your mother is coming for?"

"She's here for three days on her way to the US. Do you mind sleeping on the sofa in the living room for two nights, Mum and I can share our bed?" I wasn't sure how Benjamin would react to this and felt bad asking him, especially since he left for work at quarter to six every morning. Seeing there was no other option he could only but agree even if reluctantly.

"I don't have much choice do I, so no, I'll sleep on the sofa." Benjamin was always the practical and level headed one in our relationship.

"How do you feel about possibly being a father?" I asked after supper while we sat watching television.

"You know my feelings Emma, I'd love to be a father, but don't put pressure on yourself. Let's agree to take each day as is comes and to expect the worse. That way we'll not be disappointed." How I longed for Benjamin to just lose his head for one brief moment and say openly and unconditionally what his heart was dying to voice out loud.

Instead my husband as always guarded his true feelings, infuriating me.

We made love that night for the first time in a while. I think the London lifestyle, so full of administration, long commutes and arduous working hours, had taken their toll on our energy levels and hence our sex drives. We were spoilt, being used to permanent staff back home in South Africa and relatively very little traffic. There seemed now so little time in the day and so much more to do. I had become a housewife, a cleaning lady and an ironing lady overnight while still trying to keep abreast of my career.

Afterwards, we lay in each other's arms, now warm from our physical exertion, for a while just listening to our hearts beating in the silence of the night and I felt, as I always did when lying on Benjamin's chest, safe, secure and loved.

Friday came and I arrived for my appointment with one minute to spare. Ran to the toilet to relieve myself, an activity, which was becoming habitual.

"How have you been getting on, Mrs Hogan?" Kim asked, as I undressed and climbed onto the examination table for the scan.

"Fine, I don't enjoy the injections though, they certainly do sting and I tend to bruise for a few hours immediately afterwards."

"That's normal, nothing to be concerned about. Now, let's see what's happening with your follicles." Kim brushed over my remark. "This might feel a little uncomfortable to start, even a little cool." With that Kim lubricated the probe Dr Collins had used on my first visit and began sliding a condom over the top. As she did this with such dexterity I could not help but think how phallic it all was. As she inserted the probe I felt extremely uncomfortable and self-conscious.

"Please relax Mrs Hogan," Kim urged me.

"That's better," she said as I flinched for the last time. "Take a look at the monitor, as you can see there are many small follicles but no dominant one yet. I think we should continue until Monday with a half dose of Menopur and check again then. Did Dr Collins explain how we're conservative to begin with, which may mean it takes longer but better that than over stimulating your ovaries."

"Yes, she did thanks. Should the Menopur have had an effect already?" I asked, thinking perhaps it was my body where the problem lay once again and that normally they would have seen a response after two days of injections.

"Mrs Hogan please don't expect miracles overnight, this process may take time, sometimes a lot of time at that. There is no need to be alarmed at this point, so go home and enjoy your weekend with your husband," Kim said reassuringly.

I appreciated Kim's reassurances but I still sensed that something was not quite right. Not sure what that something was I decided not to press her, dressed, collected my stock of Menopur from the nurses – enough to last me the weekend – and left the hospital with my loyal companion: my little blue bag. I felt like a junkie carrying all these syringes and medicines around with me. I wondered on my way home on the Central line, how I'd explain these to a policeman and if he'd even believe me if I was stopped by one and was searched. I'd probably be arrested and accused of being part of the al-Qaeda network caught smuggling chemical weapons, and immediately deported!

As I fumbled in my handbag for the keys to our apartment I heard the phone ringing. Typical, just when you needed to be nimble, your coordination fails you I thought to myself. Eventually, fed up, I tipped my bag upside down onto the hallway carpet and they fell, along with everything else, to the ground.

By the time I had picked everything up and unlocked the door the phone had stopped ringing. Damn, butter fingers!

I tossed my bag onto the sofa and dialled into our answering service: "You have two new messages," the recorded voice was saying. Mum had called to confirm what time she needed to be collected the following day from Heathrow Terminal Four and the Greys who wanted to meet Benjamin and I for a light supper at our local 'Tootsies' in Holland Park.

"Hi Susan, got your message. Benjamin and I would love to meet you guys for supper. He and I are meeting at the gym and if we're up to it will do a forty-minute workout. We could meet you after that." I had rung Benjamin before calling Susan to check with him.

"Great, say around eight thirty?" Susan's husband, John, had been one of Benjamin's closest friends since they were teenagers back home. They had been living in London for four years before we moved over.

I decided not to call my mother from our home phone but to get into my gym clothes first and call on the way there from my mobile phone. That way I would not be waylaid.

"Hi Mum, got your message, I can't wait to see you," I said, as I walked down Brunswick Gardens onto Kensington Church Street to our gym just round the corner. It was half past six yet seemed like mid afternoon still. Oh, how I loved London during the summer, those long hours of uninterrupted daylight.

"Hi darling, how was your day and how is work going? What's the weather like, I've only packed lightweight cardigans?" My mother, in the habit of asking multiple questions simultaneously, never gave you enough time to answer any of them before moving onto the next topic.

"The weather is cool but pleasant, a light cardigan and slacks for evening wear is fine. You can wear a summer coat of mine if you want when we go to the theatre tomorrow night," I said, answering her last question first which I knew was most important. My mother, a very elegant lady, always dressed for every occasion, unlike her daughter, who never gave her 'outfit' a second thought until the last minute. I think sometimes I purposefully didn't plan ahead because I so didn't want to emanate my mother.

"My flight, BA 54, gets in at twenty to eight tomorrow morning at Terminal four and I depart again on Tuesday early afternoon for New York. Are you and Benjamin still going to pick me up, I can always catch the Paddington Express and you can fetch me from there instead?" My mother never travelled light and I shuddered then chuckled as I pictured her with three bags negotiating the train on her own.

"How many bags will you have with you?" I asked.

"Three and my usual vanity case. But they are not full of my clothes, there are goodies for Chris," my mother added as if guilty of a crime. Chris was my eldest brother who lived with his fiancée in New York.

"I think it'll be easier for you if Benjamin and I pick you up at the airport," I said, knowing that that was what we'd be doing all along. "What's Dad up to while you're away?"

"He's playing golf and more golf and oh, yes, there are two board meetings to attend."

"Send him hugs and kisses from me and travel safely. We'll meet you at the Starbucks." With that I entered the elevator to the third floor. Oh Dad, you need to balance your life and find another interest, one you can share with Mum in your dotage, I thought, as I exited the elevator.

I loved my exercise, but found less and less time in London to do it on a regular basis. I was taken aback when Dr Collins remarked on my uncompromising need for physical exercise almost seven days a week.

She had told me this during our last meeting.

"Hi sweetheart," as I gave Benjamin a hug, "missed you today," I whispered in his ear.

"Hi Beanbags, missed you too," he said as he kissed me, "have you confirmed plans with Susan and John for tonight?"

"Yep, Tootsies at eight thirty. Hope that works?"

"We've got forty minutes to workout then. Let's use the treadmill for twenty and then do some weights for the rest of the time, how's that sound?"

"Great."

Ben and I finished our workout, having released the endorphins we needed to and Ben managing to burn off his pent-up energy and forget about his strenuous day at work.

We reached our apartment, having run back from the gym, as if the forty-five minute workout wasn't enough! We took turns showering, pulled on a pair of jeans and a shirt and took off on foot for Tootsies.

John and Susan were already at the restaurant when we arrived a little after eight thirty. It was a beautiful evening out.

"Hey guys, great to see you," John said as he stood up from the table.

"Hi Susan, you're looking so relaxed, what's the secret?" I said as I lent over and kissed her hello.

"Oh, John and I'll tell you over dinner." With that my heart fell and I knew the answer without going any further. She was pregnant. As much as I tried to steer clear of the subject it kept raising its head as if taunting me.

We ordered dinner and began discussing our travel plans for August and September when I couldn't resist any longer.

"So back to your secret. Are you pregnant?" I asked straight out.

"Yes, John and I are thrilled. I fell pregnant the second month easy as pie." Susan sounded so overjoyed and excited. It was wonderful to see. Benjamin looked over the table at me trying to gauge my reaction; he caught my eye and winked. I felt my heart sink and my mind wander. Why is it so easy for some women and just so impossibly difficult for others? It's so unfair.

"That's wonderful news you two. Well done. How far along are you?" I hadn't noticed a tummy but looked a little more closely and oh yes, there sure enough was the start of a bulge.

"I'm sixteen weeks and have had serious morning sickness for the last three weeks."

"That's no lie," John laughed, "she's running off to the toilet every five minutes."

"You managed to get one past the goalie! Goodbye to our Friday night pub evenings, John," Benjamin interjected. He, John and four other mates regularly met on a Friday night for a couple of drinks.

"No ways, those are sacred, I'll still be there," John said jokingly and smiled at Susan who glared back.

We spent the rest of the evening talking about the baby, ultrasound scans, and hospitals everything and anything to do with parenthood and childbirth.

By the time I arrived home I was exhausted and saddened. I felt bad that at a time when I should have been full of excitement for John and Susan; I was envious.

"You did well Emma I'm proud of you," Benjamin said as he pulled me close to him and held me tightly. As I hugged him, feeling the reassurance of his warm body against mine, I began to release the tears I had succeeded all evening in hiding. We must have stood there, in the centre of our living room in the still darkness of the night with only the orange glow of the street lights shining through the large sachet windows, for at least half an hour before Benjamin whispered, "Let's go to bed darling."

Chapter Three

Saturday morning dawned and I woke to the sound of Benjamin hoovering the carpet in our living room, something he was in the habit of doing on a regular basis. His unique way of letting off steam I think!

"What time is it?" I asked in my early morning voice, barely audible

"It's a little after six o'clock. We need to leave at quarter to seven to make sure we get to Heathrow on time to collect your mother. Why don't you jump into the shower first?" Benjamin knew how long it took me to wake on the weekend and was obviously concerned about time.

"I'll put a blanket on the sofa for you and a pillow. Sorry darling, but it's only for three nights," I said with a mouth full of toothpaste.

As I changed in the bedroom I heard swearing in the bathroom. "Oh shit," John hissed.

"What's wrong?" I asked as I walked back to the bathroom.

"I hit my head on the cupboard. This bathroom is so small you can't swing a cat in here." We had moved to the UK only recently and were renting in Kensington until we found something we liked and could afford, something with space, which was almost impossible considering that we came from a country where you could fit the entire UK into our largest game reserve, the Kruger National Park.

The traffic to the airport wasn't too bad for a Saturday. We were lucky because typically the BA flights from South Africa were among the earliest to land at Heathrow. As we waited at the Starbucks for my mother to come through customs, I wondered how I was going to inject myself that evening and for the next two while my mother was staying with us.

"You'll have to do it while you run the shower and close the bathroom door," Benjamin suggested.

With that I saw my mother or should I say, what I instinctively knew was her, behind a mound of overstuffed suitcases balancing peculiarly on a small trolley, walking through the glass doors out of customs and approaching the Starbucks. You couldn't miss her! I ran to her and gave her the biggest hug ever. I hadn't seen her for two months since my last business trip to Johannesburg and I had missed my family.

"It's so good to see you Mum. How was your flight?" I asked as Benjamin tried to take her trolley from her.

"Hi darling. Fine, Benjamin I'll do that it's heavy, I'm carrying loads of stuff for Chris." My mother was so pre-occupied with what we'd think of all her luggage.

"Let me take it, you've had a long flight." Benjamin gave her a kiss on both cheeks and managed to steal the trolley away.

"You're looking good, have you put on a few pounds?" mother asked, as all mothers do, scrutinising their daughters to see if there was anything they'd missed. I silently wished that were the case and the extra pounds were baby pounds, but that wasn't to be.

"I'm not sure, haven't weighed myself recently," I lied, not wanting to pursue the subject in case Mum went on to ask about babies. But silently wondering now if I had started letting myself go.

"I've booked tickets for the ballet tonight, 'La Bayadere' at the Royal Opera House, hope you're up to it after such a long journey, it's the only night I could get." Mother loved the ballet and I thought this would be a treat.

"That's sounds lovely darling, I'm always love ballet. I've just the outfit I can wear. What time?"

"Eight o'clock. I thought we could have an early supper beforehand in Covent Garden somewhere. It'll just be the two of us."

"I'm not joining you two girls I'm afraid ballet is not my forte." I had tried to convince Benjamin to come along but no amount of bribery could get him to sit through three hours of ballet, even if it was for his mother-in-law.

"What will you do?" she asked all inquiringly.

"Oh, I've arranged to meet a few friends and we're going for a drink and then dinner."

I could see my mother was a little disappointed, so I quickly changed the subject.

"We've been looking for a house over the past few weeks, Mum. Everything is so expensive in London." I had been in touch with five estate agents and enlisted our details on their database. We had been inundated with calls and brochures of numerous properties, which told me it was a buyers market and agents were desperate to sell property. The buy-to-let market had recently been burned and real buyers with 'no chain' were a hard find.

"What are you looking for?"

"A three bedroom apartment located centrally, preferably in a complex of sorts with off-street parking. We've seen a great spot in a complex called Kensington Green." Little did I know that what I had imagined then was certainly not what we were to finally purchase for reasons still to be discovered.

"Well, if you are planning to have children the two of you, which by the way I advise you two should start to think about soon, you will need more space." My mother had raised the dreaded subject.

"Mmm, I see your point," I said ending the conversation there.

"I didn't realise you lived so centrally. I used to live around the corner in Notting Hill, in a small apartment in

Ladbroke Grove." My mother had lived and worked in London for many years before she married my father.

"Yes, it only takes us twenty minutes on the central line to get to St Paul's in the City." Both Benjamin and I worked within a few blocks of one another, which meant that some evenings we travelled home together on the tube. After a seriously long day at the office, having usually left for work in the dark and seen little sunlight all day, it was refreshing to meet Benjamin and have someone to talk to and laugh with on the ride home, catching up with each other's day.

"Mum, you and I will be sleeping in the same bed, Benjamin has opted for the sofa." Mum immediately looked at Benjamin.

"No need to worry, Judy, I'll be fine and prefer to sleep on the sofa, it gives me a much needed break from Emma!" Benjamin said jokingly, or at least I hoped so, to reassure Mum.

Mum and I spent the rest of the morning catching up and unpacking while Benjamin went to swim at the gym. We then all went for a walk in Hyde Park stopping off at a nearby Prêt a Manger for a coffee and a sandwich before returning home late afternoon.

That evening I suggested that Mum shower first and that she and Benjamin go down for a drink at our local pub and that I'd join them later. Mum and I could then go on to Covent Garden by cab and Benjamin could join his friends.

"No darling, I'll wait for you here," Mum protested. She wasn't going to make this easy for me.

"Judy, the pub round the corner is new and has a friendly atmosphere, Emma won't be long but it'll give you and I a chance to catch up on our own." Clever thinking Benjamin!

"Oh, all right." Mum and Benjamin left the apartment while I was still in my bath towel. I quickly prepared the medication and placed the syringe into the plunger; my hands were clammy and I felt nervous administering the injection without Benjamin around. He had sat next to me on the sofa every evening until now for support as I jabbed myself in the thigh. Funny, I thought, just how useless one could feel when alone. As I released the plunger I realised I had held it too close to the surface of the skin so the needle penetrated deeper than usual. Ouch! As I pulled the plunger away my leg bled more than usual and the skin started to turn a bluish colour. I was rushing, so this served me right I suppose.

By the time I joined my mother and Benjamin, he was onto his second beer.

"What took you so long, we're going to be late for the ballet?" she asked concerned.

"Oh, Chris phoned from New York and wanted to check your travel schedule and generally catch up," I lied, but knew she would then drop the subject and ask after my brother.

"How's Chris? Was he in San Francisco on business this week? Did you speak to Haley?" Bombarded by a million questions I chose to answer the first and move on.

"Chris sends his love, he and Haley can't wait to see you. How have you and Benjamin been getting along?"

"Darling, I think you and your mother should start to make your way to Covent Garden. It's getting late, you'll probably only have time for a finger supper now at the Opera House." Benjamin settled the bill and we left the pub as quickly as I had entered it just a few moments before. I didn't think that Mum had suspected anything but I felt uncomfortable lying none-the-less.

As we entered the Royal Opera House I felt her hug my arm and then whisper in my ear, "Thanks darling, this is extra special." Ballet was a quintessential part of my mother's world. I felt a sense of pride in my foresight for arranging this outing.

The ballet was outstanding. India being the setting, such an exotic country, served as an excellent catalyst to escape from the hundreds of thoughts about work and fertility that were constantly consuming my mind. I found myself relaxing as I switched off and focused on nothing else but the beautiful Daria Pavlenko, who played Nikiya the Indian temple dancer and Andrian Fadeyev, the noble warrior, Solar.

"The costumes are spectacular," Mum said as the curtain fell for interval, "let's get a drink outside in the foyer."

"Good idea," I said, and just as I was about to stand up, my skirt moved ever so slightly.

"What's that bruise on your leg?" Mum asked having caught sight of one of my previous injection sites lower down on my thigh.

"Oh that. That's and old bruise that just doesn't seem to fade," I lied.

"I've got some arnica, you can use some when we get home and I suggest we get you some," Mum said as we got up from our seats and made our way to the bar.

We stood as we drank our lime and sodas and ate a small plate of cucumber sandwiches.

"How is work going?"

"Not bad, marketing any company in these times is difficult especially a newcomer in this market. We are trying to change our image and move into a new more profitable sector of the market, but we are competing against the big fish who have been around for years." I skimmed over the detail, it was too complicated to discuss and I wouldn't do it justice in the five minutes of the interval remaining.

"Benjamin said that you have thought about joining Dad in September in Scotland and that you think it is a good idea. How long do you think you can get away for and could you spend time at St Andrews with Dad, it would be so good for Benjamin?" My mother really wanted us to get out of London for a while and relax since we hadn't taken a day's leave for ten months. We had even gone to the extreme in arranging our move from South African to coincide with a Bank Holiday weekend in the UK so as not to miss a day's work. We were what you would call 'peculiar'.

Thinking about it all now as she spoke, made me realise just how tired I actually was. Moving countries and offices and trying to set up had proved a far greater challenge than I was prepared to admit.

"Yes, we would love to see Scotland and this gives us an opportunity to see St Andrews. Benjamin can play the Old Course with Dad." My father was a member of the Royal and Ancient. Benjamin could play the course by invitation through Dad, something he had silently wanted to do for a while now.

The bell to signal that intermission was over and the second act was about to begin began ringing, so we downed the last bit of our drinks and made our way back to our seats.

The third and fourth acts were as colourful and spectacular as the first; the Kingdom of the Shades in Act III was the highlight for me.

It was late by the time we left the Opera House and hailed a cab.

"It's half past eleven already," I said, as we sat in the back of the black cab on our way to Kensington.

"Oh thank you, I've never seen 'La Bayadere' danced by the Royal Ballet, it was really special," she said as she squeezed my hand.

I hadn't once thought of the fertility treatment during the entire evening, so, selfishly I had enjoyed it because it had helped carry my mind far away from current problems.

I was really tempted in that moment of closeness to tell Mum about the treatment and to ask for her support.

"Mum?" I said as the cab drove into our street.

"Yes love," she said.

"Oh nothing," changing my mind.

"Is Aunt Viv alright?"

"Why?" Mum seemed to avoid answering my question.

"No real reason, just... I speak to her often and she sounded different the other day when I called," I said.

"In what way," Mum said.

"Distant, as if she wasn't really listening to what I was saying."

"Well, we all grow old you know and she's eighty-seven this year, but yes, she's going a little senile and is forgetful. Don't be surprised if she calls you by another name," Mum said as we stepped out of the cab, paid the driver and made our way to the apartment.

Benjamin was asleep on the sofa in the living room when we arrived home. So we tiptoed into the bedroom closed the door and changed, then turned the light off and tiptoed into the bathroom, brushed our teeth and tiptoed back to the bedroom, climbed into our tiny double bed together and fell sound asleep. This was the first time I had ever slept in the same bed as her. Even as children my parents' bed was sacred and we weren't allowed near it. As I closed my eyes, lying next to Mum, I felt an odd sense of security.

Sunday morning and our apartment was unusually still. All three of us must have been exhausted as no one had stirred and it was ten o'clock by the time I strolled through into the living room to see what Benjamin was up to. Work had been quite stressful for him of late and seemed to sap him of energy, so that by the end of each week he was like a run down vehicle in need of a service. I hadn't gotten lucky for weeks! Just as well, I thought, he'd have enough of me when the time came and we were told we had to have intercourse whether he wanted to or not. He'd have to perform on demand!

I lent over and kissed him. As I did this, his eyes opened and he smiled and pulled me back for another kiss this time longer and more passionate. "What time is it?" His eyes betrayed him, I realised he hadn't necessarily slept so late due to work pressures but more likely due to an almighty hangover brought about by the 'boys'.

"Your eyes look like Blood River. Did you have a good night with the guys?" I asked knowing that he would not be in the mood for dealing with an obnoxious wife.

"It was fun, we had dinner at Nobu, Gavin was able to get us a table." Nobu is one of the most famous Japanese restaurants in London and almost impossible to get a table unless you booked four weeks in advance.

"Did you sit at Gavin's regular table then?" I asked.

"Yep, great evening." Benjamin seemed relaxed.

I knew about Gavin's infamous table, it was usually in bird's eye view of the bar that was always packed with would-be models waiting to be discovered. I twinged knowing that Ben had probably been goggle-eyed all night.

"I'm jealous, we'll have to arrange another time to eat there when I can join you. The ballet was fantastic! I just switched off. Mum loved it and I felt really good about having organised something I knew she'd enjoy and remember."

I heard the toilet flush, which meant Mum, was up and about.

"How did you sleep Mum?" I asked

"Fine, a little cramped but not too bad. How long have you been up?"

"Not long. Thought we could shower up and walk down to our local Starbucks, grab a muffin and a cappuccino and then drive through to Wimbledon and walk in Wimbledon Park. We'll show you two homes we have seen for sale and are quite interested in." Wimbledon presented an ideal location for Benjamin and I as the commute to the City was a mere fifteen minutes by fast train into Waterloo Station and from there Benjamin could catch the Bank line and I the 525 bus to Holborn. Only issue was price of course. Why was it that there always had to be a compromise?

"How was your evening Benjamin?" Mum asked.

"Fine thanks." Benjamin clearly wasn't in the mood to elaborate.

"Oh, tell me about the food, I hear it's one of the best Japanese restaurants this side of the Atlantic," Mum continued.

"I've heard that also."

As usual the smell of the coffee beans from Starbucks beckoned us. This morning it was extremely busy and I was concerned we wouldn't get a table outside in the courtyard; on such a beautiful morning it would be a shame to have to sit inside.

Benjamin took our orders and went to stand in the queue while Mum and I scouted outside for a table.

"Are these seats taken?" I asked a young man sitting on his own.

"No, go ahead," he answered. "I'd be delighted if you'd join me."

Had he misunderstood my intentions? I quickly added, "My husband will be joining us shortly." Not being used to men approaching me as Benjamin was usually with me, I suddenly blushed. I must admit it made me feel really good though. I had found being married had changed Benjamin's regard for me slightly. Where had the flattery gone, a core ingredient of any love affair?

Benjamin joined us with muffins and cappuccinos in hand and as he did so the gentleman sitting at the table finished his coffee and go up to go.

"I hope we're not intruding?" Benjamin said.

"No not at all, I was on my way before your wife asked if you could take these vacant seats." With that the gentleman left.

"I hear there's a fabulous Giorgio Armani exhibition on in the City right now. Shall we go?"

"Oh, I just love his designs, yes I'd love to," Mum said, and we planned on going the following day.

I heard the shower running and turned over to look at my clock, it was five o'clock and Benjamin was already up. I slipped out of the bed from under the covers trying not to wake Mum and tiptoed to the bathroom.

"Morning, why are you up so early?" I asked knowing that Benjamin usually left for work at six o'clock and only needed twenty minutes to get dressed in the mornings unlike me of course. Men had it easy, they didn't have to be creative first thing in the morning. All they had to do was choose a shirt and tie and put on a work suit. Women on the other hand spent hours trying to figure out what to wear, depending on what type of meetings were taking place that day and who they needed to impress. All that colour coding mumbo jumbo.

"I couldn't sleep, the sofa's so uncomfortable. I might as well get up and get into the office and be productive. I've been watching Bloomberg's for the last half hour anyway." If I left Benjamin alone in front of the television for even a minute, he'd change the channel and be glued to Bloomberg's.

"I've got an appointment with Dr Collins today. I thought I'd see if Mum could spend the morning with Vivien and then we'd meet up for lunch and go on to the Armani exhibition. I've told Mum that I need to go into the office for one meeting today even though I've taken two days' leave." Vivien was an old school friend of my mother's who had been living in London for fifteen years.

"I'm sure it'll work out fine." Benjamin was not really interested in the logistics, his mind was in the office already and focused on share prices, so I kissed him and went back to bed.

"Mrs Hogan your follicles are still relatively small, so we'll now increase the dosage of gonadtrophins," Dr Collins said, as she scrutinised the image on the ultrasound screen.

I lent forward to see what was going on and all I could see looked to me like a cluster of small white spots and two large sac-like structures, which were obviously my ovaries. One needed X-ray lenses to really decipher the image correctly or of course a trained eye.

"Do you think this is problematic?" I asked apprehensively. I wasn't sure what to expect but this just seemed to be another disappointment.

"No. It is not unusual not to see a response yet. The dosage we gave initially was low as I said at the start, so I half expected that we'd need to up the dosage before we'd see a response." Dr Collins seemed calm and this reassured me, at least for the time being.

"We'll increase the dose to a full one for the next three days and again see how we go. Please come back on Thursday morning for another scan." Dr Collins then said something to Lucy but I couldn't make out exactly what she was saying.

"Lucy, is everything alright?" I asked not sure if I really wanted to know the answer.

"Yes, Mrs Hogan, just relax. Your body has not been functioning correctly for years now, it will take time for the natural cycle to return and for your body to interpret the signals and respond positively." Lucy too sounded calm and confident.

If I thought about the weeks that had passed since the start of fertility treatment they all seemed to blur into one. Each day was the same as the day before and going to be the same as the next, like running on a treadmill versus running on the road outside, you never passed an unexpected tree you hadn't seen while running the day before. The route never changed. It was stamina that counted in the end, perhaps that was what would get me through this too?

Chapter Four

Tuesday morning came all too soon. I had dropped mother off at Paddington Station to catch the Heathrow Express, always the quickest way into Heathrow Airport. It didn't matter that Mum had three heavy suitcases because we checked these in at Paddington Station before she boarded the train. Walking back to my car I felt a sudden sense of loss, loneliness even despair. We had spent three special days together and I wondered if I would ever have the opportunity to share such extraordinary memories with my own daughter or even son for that matter. I felt a sudden panic attack.

Suddenly I heard my phone ringing. "Hello." I was not expecting a call.

"Hi, Emma, you're needed in the office. Can you come in and present to a prospective client?" It was Mark my boss. Oh drat I had planned to go for a run in the park and then relax in a long bath and do my nails. That was the end of that.

"Sure, what time and whose the client?" I was used to off the cuff presentations and dropping previous plans in the line of duty, so the request didn't bother me as much as it intrigued me as to who it was Mark was referring to.

"Oh, Coopers and Co. the logistics company who are looking to roll-out a common alliance methodology in all their offices around the world. It's a big deal if we can get it. We're presenting to their Board at six o'clock." Nothing like a little bit of pressure to get my head spinning. My adrenalin pumping I looked at my watch.

"It's three o'clock. I'll see you in an hour so we can discuss and prepare our presentation and marketing approach. Can you make sure the sales director is around for an hour or so beforehand to prepare. Is this our first formal presentation or have you already met with them?" Mark was a fantastic marketer and his good looks and charismatic aura usually immediately won a prospective client's trust.

"It's the first formal one, put it that way," Mark said.

"You're not setting me up for failure are you?" I asked jokingly of course.

"No just testing your nerve."

"Darling," I said to Benjamin when he picked up the phone, "I'm going to be late tonight I've been called into the office for a client presentation. There's some salmon in the fridge and stuff for a salad and I've just taken out some frozen roast potatoes which will need baking." We shared the cooking most evenings, so it wasn't unusual for Benjamin to have to get dinner prepared for both of us. We often only ate at around nine o'clock anyway.

"I'll manage dinner but did you remind them that you had taken leave today?" Benjamin did not like the firm I worked for, particularly as they were in the habit of calling me in over a weekend or getting me to cancel vacation time.

"Yep, they'll credit today back. Don't say what I know you're thinking. I'll speak to them and let them know they can't keep calling me in at the last minute like this." I had promised Benjamin to speak to Mark about this for some time, but just hadn't got round to doing so. I secretly liked the fact that they needed me.

I eventually arrived home at eight thirty exhausted and guilty for having neglected Benjamin; this wasn't the first time either. I knew in my heart of hearts that this would need to change and if we were to have a child I could not work the hours I had been until now.

"Hi, sweetheart." I tried to sound energetic and up beat so as not to fuel Benjamin's already angry disposition towards the company's lack of consistency in their policies and procedures.

"Mmm, does your company know anything about family values?" Benjamin was pissed off and wasn't going to let me off lightly this time.

"I'm sorry I know how you feel and I'll do something about it this week, promise."

"You've said that before Emma. You are going to have to make a choice sometime soon, you can't expect to be a good mother and work the hours you're forced to work right now." He forgot to add 'wife and mother'.

There wasn't much I could say and I didn't have the energy to pursue the conversation.

"Can we discuss this some other time? I'd like to spend a couple of hours before bed time with you quietly over dinner without arguing," I said.

"Emma, I'll drop the subject because I know you're tired, but don't let work dictate your life. I'm sure it's got something to do with your fertility problems."

That was hard to swallow. He had stepped over the line with that one.

Although we both knew that the stress of work and the unhealthy hours were certainly not helping, it was cruel to throw this at me.

'I'm sorry Emma, you just know how this issue gets to me," Ben said as he tried to hug me and make up.

I couldn't help it, I just loved feeling in control and work was one area where the more pressure there was, the more I seemed to thrive. It wasn't going to be long before life taught me a lesson or two about my obsession with work. While I might have been thriving in one sense, in another I was withering and so were those close to me.

I administered the injection; we ate dinner together and while watching television I fell asleep in Benjamin's arms.

I hadn't realised the heartache I was inflicting upon my husband, he never said a word so I just kept at him relentlessly. The one man in my life I loved more than anything was the one I was hurting most.

I had managed to secure a five thirty appointment with Dr Collins on Thursday so I didn't have to leave work too early. Feeling rather apprehensive as I hoped the dosage of gonatrophins had worked, I had been to the toilet twice in ten minutes. At least if I did fall pregnant I would be used to a bladder that required constant attention!

"Why isn't the medication working?" I asked as Dr Collins broke the news again that the dosage had not worked. I felt desperate, the only thoughts and images running through my mind were visual images of IVF and thousands of needles, having to give up work and even worse, perhaps being told I couldn't have children and the best would be to give up and adopt.

"Now Mrs Hogan I am not saying that the medication will not work, all I'm saying is that the dosage is not quite enough." I was impatient and in all honesty I hadn't banked on it taking longer than the first cycle. I thought all along that this, like all the challenges I had faced in life, would be easily overcome.

I had been wrong; Mother Nature, I was learning had control over me and not the other way round. Was Mother Nature telling me something and was I not listening hard enough?

I decided to call Phoebe.

"Hi Phoebe, have you got a moment?" I asked knowing that I had called Phoebe at work.

"Hi Emma, yes I'm sitting at my desk. How are things going?" Phoebe worked three days a week for an investment bank in the City. She had told me once how thrilled she was on a Monday morning knowing she would have three days away from the kids. Time for herself and time to be Phoebe and not Mummy. She also told me in the same breath that come every Wednesday, she was just as thrilled knowing she was going to be at home with her children for four days. This was the mental conundrum that consumed many a mother.

"Not that well really." I felt the first tear drop run down my cheek, then the second and third and I was history after that. A long pause followed which allowed me to get over the crying bout. "They've increased the dosage of medication now three times; my body doesn't seem to respond. I'm, well, I'm wondering if my dream of having a child may not come true, even with help."

"Emma, relax my friend. Everything will be fine it will just take time. Dr Collins is one of the best I'm sure she won't let you down. Did you know that I had a miscarriage the first attempt?" No, I had no idea; I had thought it was plain sailing for her.

"No, I had no idea. When was that, Phoebe?" I was shocked but at the same time relieved that it wasn't so simple for most people.

"Right before I had the twins. The first cycle worked and I fell pregnant with one child but at the ten week scan my body had absorbed the embryo." Phoebe sounded in control but a quiver in her voice gave away a hint of the devastation she and Richard must have felt at the time.

"I'm so sorry." What could I say; here I was selfishly thinking of my own problems trying to seek comfort from Phoebe when I did not realise that she had gone through this without my knowing.

"I'm blessed Emma, I have two wonderful children for which I am eternally grateful."

I felt ashamed. My world felt as if it was tumbling down around me, I was so consumed by the desire to have a child, that I had lost perspective. I was not alone in my plight, there were many women out there who had difficulties, and some even experienced the immense joy of falling pregnant, like Phoebe, and then suffered the misfortune of losing it before full term. I needed to stop feeling sorry for myself.

"Emma, let's get together for lunch in Wimbledon next week Saturday. The guys can play golf and you and I can chat, do some window-shopping and have a girl's day out. How's that sound?"

"Just what I need, I think. Will you get Richard to call Benjamin to arrange golf?" Richard was a member of the Royal Wimbledon Golf Club.

I also so wanted to talk to Aunt Viv; usually she would have consoled me and made everything seem all right, but it wasn't the same any more. She'd lost touch with the here and now and the only glimpse I had of her old self was when she spoke of the past.

I administered the injections every day for the next three days over the weekend as usual, except that I seemed to sense an increased fear and doubt in my mind as to whether or not it would have the desired effect. Benjamin was marvellous, he provided me with the energy and enthusiasm to remain optimistic and to appreciate all the other aspects of our life. He succeeded in making me smile. We made an effort to keep busy. Benjamin arranged for us to go to the movies, to have dinner and drinks with friends and to run each morning before breakfast in the park. We even spent three hours looking at possible apartments in London – anything and everything to keep my mind off of the fertility treatment.

Sitting quietly on the sofa on Sunday playing Backgammon, I turned to Benjamin. Running my fingers through his hair I told him how much he meant to me.

"I know that everything's going to be fine. I have you don't I?" I said.

"Emma, you're holding up well."

Early the following morning just after Benjamin left for work, the phone rang.

"Emma, Emma?" It was Aunt Viv on the phone.

"Viv, what's the matter?" I asked concerned.

"Mmm, yes I can't remember why I called exactly but didn't you say something about babies the other day. Are you having one?" she asked extremely flustered.

"It's alright Viv, I did say something along those lines but I'm still trying so no babies yet, you'll just have to sit tight and wait," I said, tears trickling down my cheek as I realised Mum hadn't told me everything. Viv was clearly going downhill fast and she wanted to protect me.

"I think I'm losing my marbles, Emma, but don't tell anyone will you?" Her plea for help came across as a surprise. I had always been the one needing her help, now she needed mine and I wasn't there to be with her.

"You, never! Those shiny marbles are burning brighter than ever. I'll be back in South Africa for Christmas and we can go for long walks like old times together," I said, knowing that Viv wasn't really getting out much any longer.

"Emma-Beez, I miss you. I think I've lost my way," Viv said and my heart sank.

"Emma, have you got an hour free today to meet?" Mark asked as I walked into the office on Monday morning. He looked rather pleased with himself and I wondered what was going on.

"Sure, I'm free around lunchtime, let's grab a sandwich and meet over lunch. I'll book us a boardroom."

I ran out just before lunch and grabbed a sandwich from the deli around the corner and, passing an Ottakars, I couldn't resist asking where they kept their books on motherhood and pregnancy.

I stashed the book I had bought, *Birth and Beyond,* into my cupboard at my desk and took my sandwich into the boardroom for my meeting with Mark. No one at the company knew about my fertility treatment and that's the way I wanted to keep it.

"So, what's up Mark?" I asked very casually not putting two and two together.

"I've got good news and bad news; which do you want to hear first?" Why was there rarely an occasion when good news existed without a proviso?

"Give me the good news first please."

"We've been awarded the Coopers and Co. contract in conjunction with one of the big fish, yet to be disclosed, who will project manage the entire installation. It's worth twenty million pounds over five years to us." Mark was ecstatic; this would help him earn his stripes in the company.

"Congratulations, that's great news. Who has been assigned as Account Executive?" I asked wondering who would manage such a prestigious account.

"Emma, first I want to thank you for your presentation the other evening, I think that helped to seal the account. Now the bad news is, they want you on their account. I know you have requested we reduce the demands on your time, but this is a fantastic opportunity for you and could make your career. What do you say?" Mark really wanted me to say yes there and then, but as much as I wanted to, as this would be a move upwards promising larger bonuses, something inside me was saying no. I had reached a crossroads in my career and I had a choice to make, the consequences would be great either way and I knew it.

"Mark, I'm flattered but may I have some time to think this through? It not only involves a change in direction but also an additional demand on my time. I'm going to have to speak to Benjamin. How soon does the client need to know?"

"Tomorrow." Mark was uncompromising.

"I can't give you an answer tomorrow, I can promise an answer by Friday though. You'll have to stall the client." I wanted to see if this dose of medication had started to take effect finally and if so this would be my cue. I already knew what Benjamin would say.

"Fine, I'll find some legitimate excuse," Mark said.

"Emma, you have to make a choice. I'll support you either way, but you can't have the best of both worlds. Either you are prepared to forgo fertility for now and progress your career or you decide to slow down career wise, for now at least, and focus on nurturing your body and committing yourself to the fertility programme." Benjamin was stern in his view, but spoke softly, knowing that this would be one of the hardest decisions to make.

If I refused to take up the position of account executive for the client it would be indicative of my priorities and would probably hamper my career. If I chose to take up the position, which would be a promotion in terms of salary, bonus and status within the company, I might just jeopardise my fertility programme. Time would not permit me to give one hundred percent to both at the same level of intensity and neither would my body.

"I'm torn Benjamin. I know what my decision should be, but it still doesn't make it an easy one. I've worked hard for this and deserve it. When will it be the right time to start a family?"

"You know as well as I do Emma, there is no right time. You have to take the step and go with the flow from there." Benjamin at times was so pragmatic it made me sick.

"I'm going to wait and see what happens at my next scan on Wednesday. If the follicles are growing then it's a sign and if not then it's a sign too." Hadn't I lectured Benjamin at the start about commitment and focus and wasn't I the one now who was faltering?

'Don't tell me Emma, your backing down already?" Benjamin asked.

"I didn't say that, all I'm suggesting is that perhaps it isn't the right time that's all."

"You blow hot and cold you know. One minute you're lecturing me about commitment, the next you're vacillating. I don't know what you want from me, when you change your mind the whole time. I'll tell you what Emma, leave me a note every morning on the front door telling me if you are pro work or pro babies, that way when I get home from work I'll know what to say."

"What's that in the bag?" Benjamin noticed my Ottakars bag.

"Nothing. You can be so mean sometimes," I said, tears in my eyes.

"Emma, you're your own worst enemy. Is that a book?"

"Yes."

Hoping he'd not pursue it, but as I said this he opened the plastic bag and found the *Birth and Beyond* book I had bought earlier that day.

"Emma, don't get your hopes up; let's wait until you are pregnant before buying loads of books. You're only setting yourself up for disappointment."

My hands were wet with perspiration and my stomach felt ill. My mind was processing the alternatives over and over again. What if this dosage hadn't worked? What if it had? I was full of exhilarated joy one moment and despair the next as I went from one outcome to the next.

"Come through. Lucy will be with you shortly."

I undressed as usual, felt rather more exposed than I had before. Covering myself with a white sheet I sat there for what seemed like an eternity. Eventually Lucy arrived, by which time my legs were covered in little goose bumps.

"Mrs Hogan, how are you?" Lucy asked, as she opened the door and drew the curtain behind her.

"To be honest I've felt better. I'm nervous."

"Don't be. Now let's see what's going on today." Lucy watched the screen as she moved the probe around inside me. I couldn't see the screen at the angle I was lying so asked her:

"What can you see?"

"Oh, I'm sorry." Lucy adjusted the screen so I could get a better view. "I'm pleased to say that there is one follicle which has grown and it measures 15mm in diameter. Well done! Let me call Dr Collins in to give her opinion." Dr Collins would need to give the go ahead for ovulation induction.

"Good to see you again, Mrs Hogan," Dr Collins said as she entered the room.

"Yes, likewise."

"I think we might have the right dosage, after many weeks of what I know has seemed like one disappointment after the next. Your patience has paid off Mrs Hogan."

"Excellent!" Dr Collins said after studying the monitor for a while. "So it took a dose of one and a half Menopur to jolt the system just enough to get going. What we'll do now is continue on this dose for another two days and then induce ovulation if the follicle continues to grow. This is usually a sign that the egg is healthy too. Can you come in on Saturday?"

"Yes, absolutely!" I was stunned.

"Guess what?" I said, as I called Benjamin my heart pounding.

"What?" Benjamin was continuing a conversation in the background with another colleague in the office.

"It's worked, the follicles have responded and there is a dominant one at 15mm. I need to continue with injections until Saturday when they'll induce ovulation. You'll have to warm up as we'll be in for an energetic weekend." I was overwhelmed with excitement.

"Emma, that's great news. Sure I'm up for it just name the place, date and time." Benjamin sounded relieved; we had overcome the first hurdle.

"Hi Mum. What's up?" Mum had called while I was out and left an urgent message.

"Emma, this will be hard for you I know, but we've, your uncle and I that is, have thought long and hard about this and we've decided to admit Aunt Viv into a nursing home. Jim can't look after her anymore, it's too much responsibility and she needs twenty-four hour care." The news didn't surprise me, but it did sadden me. I knew our conversations would no longer be spontaneous, they would become strained and uneasy as Viv slipped into her own world and slowly started to shut out the one we shared.

"Is it that bad?" I asked.

"I'm afraid so. She can still remember who you are, but has begun to live in her past and only talks about bygone days, especially Bobby," Mum said.

"Oh Mum, I wish I were there to give you a hug and to see her. Will they take good care of her?" I asked now struck by the reality of the situation.

I dreaded nursing homes for the elderly they were depressing.

"She's in good hands," Mum said.

"How can I reach her then?" I asked, wondering if I could call her at the nursing home.

"You will have to ring the reception desk and see if they can take the phone to her," Mum said.

"I feel like my umbilical cord has just been cut," I said. Mum knew how close we were.

"I know, I know darling, life's cruel sometimes, but she's safe and as happy as anyone in her situation can be."

Benjamin drove me to Grafton Way on Saturday morning and waited outside in a parking lot around the corner from the hospital.

"You sure you don't need me to come in with you?" Benjamin asked, as I climbed out of our vehicle overwrought with emotion.

"Positive, I'll be fine it won't take long they said."

The hospital was quieter than usual and the Assisted Conception Unit was empty. I began to wonder if anyone was there when the head of the department appeared from one of the offices.

"Mrs Hogan?" he asked. I had seen him before but had never actually met him personally.

"Yes. Dr Collins asked me to come in today for ovulation induction." I hesitated expecting to see Dr Collins.

'I might have the time wrong. I thought Dr Collins had said today."

"That's right. Dr Collins asked me to administer the injection for you as I'm here today at the hospital." He sounded calm and sincere. "This shouldn't take long. I would like to take a look at the follicle first and make sure we're on track. If you would come this way and undress from the waist down please and get up onto the examination table."

I had stripped down to my knickers too many times already to be fussed by his request.

"It's grown quite a bit hasn't it?" I was full of hope and anticipation and could not help showing it.

"Yes, it's grown from 15mm to 22mm and so we can go ahead with induction of ovulation, if you approve of course?" Whoopee, I thought to myself, and a huge smile appeared across my face.

"Fine," I said cool, calm and collectedly.

"I have to inject you in your bottom, are you alright with that?" Oh no, how embarrassing. It's one thing undressing in front of a stranger and allowing him to examine you in your most private areas but it's another to expose your rear end right in front of a stranger's nose! 'Flashing a Brown Eye' suddenly took on a completely new meaning for me.

"Yes I suppose," I lied, but what choice did I have.

"Please bend a little further over." I was embarrassed and therefore had not bent over fully, which was making it difficult for him. "What are you and you husband going to do today it's such lovely weather?" he asked.

What a question at a time like this? My dentist always did the same thing: asked questions just as he shoved the suction pipe down my throat. How they expect you to carry on a conversation I don't know!

"Oh, we'll probably have lunch with friends in Portobello Road and then go for a run or walk this afternoon, nothing special. Tomorrow we may continue our search for an apartment. Ouch!" Just then he jabbed my bum.

Great; he succeeded in getting me to concentrate on something else and in that brief millisecond he jabbed me. What a cheat!

"You're good," I said jokingly.

"Thanks, it's my first time at administering an injection like this." He was just joking of course, so I decided to humour him and play along.

"Well, thank goodness you didn't tell me that at the beginning I might have called a doctor."

"Right, now as you know it is very important for you and your spouse to have intercourse today and for the next three days when you're most fertile." Intercourse sounded so formal.

"Is that once a day or more than once a day?" I asked naively.

"Oh, once a day is enough. Sperm can survive in the vagina for up to forty-eight hours, but if you're having fun it's up to you. Then comes the long wait, two weeks before you'll know." He was smiling silently to himself; my question had obviously amused him.

"You're good to go now. Good luck, we'll be holding thumbs!"

I bolted down the stairs and out into the street heading towards the car park when I remembered I had left my handbag behind. I dashed back up the stairwell, taking two stairs at a time.

"That was quick," Benjamin said when I reached the car.

"I know. I was so embarrassed he had to inject me in my bum!" Only now did I feel a little tender.

"Aah! You've got a great looking bum so don't panic." I gently punched Benjamin on the forearm.

"You're going to have to make love to me all weekend and for the next week," I exaggerated.

"You'll finish me before I'm forty." We laughed spontaneously. The pent up tension we had both been harbouring for weeks now, seemed to disappear momentarily.

Early that evening as I climbed out of the shower and stood in front of the small mirror in our tiny bathroom, Benjamin walked in and stood behind me. I could hear his breath against my ear. At first he began to massage my back and shoulders, moving his hands gently over my body, caressing it with his tender touch. He then lent down and kissed the nape of my neck as I turned to face him. We stood there for a while kissing each other then moving slowly into the bedroom.

As we made love it seemed as if we were entering a deeper level of communication with one another. His lovemaking was more intense than usual yet incredibly tender, we were no longer just having sex in order to satisfy our sexual impulse. Our lovemaking had taken on a new meaning; we were not just fooling around, we were trying to conceive our first child.

Once it was all over I put my legs behind my head and lay on my back like a trapeze artist for ten minutes to keep Benjamin's semen from running out. I must have looked like one of those contortionists. This was worse than yoga. I don't know why I did this, but I had seen it somewhere in one of those trashy magazines before and thought I might try it.

I came down from my pose and we lay naked together on the bed holding hands enjoying the silence.

"I'm starving, aren't you?" I suddenly realised I hadn't eaten a thing since lunch and our run in the park.

"Mmm," Benjamin was sleepy, typical I thought. He always fell asleep contented after sex. "What did you have in mind?" he said, kissing my inner thigh.

"I thought I'd order some Sushi. I'll pop down to 'Yo Shushi'. I'm not in the mood for playing housewife and cooking dinner tonight."

"Sounds good to me. I'll turn the television on and warm the sofa while you're out." Benjamin was content. He wasn't about to budge.

"Fine, but next time's your turn. Deal?"

"Deal." Benjamin chuckled as he got up to shower and put on a T-Shirt and some shorts.

As the water from the shower trickled down my face, my back, my entire body, I felt re-energised. Can you imagine if our lovemaking produced a child?

We spent a memorable weekend together and even identified two apartments within the same area, one of which we put in a cheeky offer for.

Chapter Five

Meanwhile, Mark, had given me until Monday to reply to the company's proposal. Friday's results had sealed my decision and I knew I had no choice. Nature was telling me something and I was going to listen this time, even if it was hard to say goodbye to such a prestigious promotion.

"Mark, I've made up my mind about the position of Account Executive for Coopers and Co. Do you have a moment to chat alone?" I asked Mark first thing Monday morning.

"Sure, just give me a minute I need to make one quick phone call first. Grab the Greenacres Boardroom, I'll meet you there in a jiffy."

I sat looking out the window while waiting for Mark, which was unusual. I never daydreamed but of late I seemed to lose concentration at work and my mind would wander into the world of motherhood, pregnancy and childbirth. Everywhere I went I noticed pregnant women and women with their small babies – the city was teeming with new mums and mums-to-be.

"Emma, Emma?" Mark was leaning across the fourteen-seater boardroom table calling to me.

"Oh, sorry Mark, lost in my own world for a moment there." It was going to be hard telling Mark. He had always been an ardent supporter of mine, but it had to be done.

"I've deliberated long and hard over the past few days and spoken at length to Benjamin about the position of Account Executive for Coopers and Co." I paused a moment to make sure I had the words right in my head before speaking further. "And I've made a decision. I'm not going to take on the role, although I am honoured to have been offered the position."

Mark looked stunned; I think he had thought I'd automatically take up the position.

"Why Emma might I ask?"

"A number of reasons." I wasn't going to mention the fertility stuff, at least not for now. "Benjamin and I hardly see each other, he travels as much as I do and our schedules never seem to coincide, we are passing ships in the night. It's taking its toll on our relationship and my health. One of us has to slow down and we may want to start a family in the near future." I used the word 'may' on purpose.

"If I took up the position I would be travelling more than I am now and to further destinations around the world. I would feel more pressure to bring in target revenues each month and to grow an already large account. There are at least three others in the company who I know wanted the position and they would be watching me eager to see if I slipped up and would waste no time in trying to find fault with my management of the account. I don't think I'm up for this level of politicking." Everything I said thus far was true; the company was highly competitive and cut-throat. The directors always backed two hungry, ambitious employees on any initiative in case they needed to reverse a decision.

"I've never known you to shy away from a challenge Emma. What's really up?" Mark was a family man too and he obviously sensed something deeper.

"I'm more than happy to continue in my current position. I enjoy a senior level within the firm. My heart's not in it, someone else who will really give it one hundred percent attention, one hundred percent of the time is more suited for the role Mark."

"What can I say Emma. I'm disappointed and so will the client be." Mark got up to leave the room and as he did so my heart fell, everything I had been building in the company over the past three years would crumble and I knew my career from now on would be stunted.

"Oh Emma, mark my words, you are making a mistake."
These were Mark's last words on the subject and they came
at me like a knife cutting the air.

"I'm exhausted, do we have to make love tonight. Surely
Saturday, Sunday, tomorrow and Wednesday will be enough?
I need a break tonight I'm bushed." It was Monday evening
and I was reminding or rather nagging Benjamin that we had
to make love again tonight.

"Why is it that when you don't want to make love to a
man they're all over you like a nappy rash and when you do
and you initiate, a man loses interest?" I asked facetiously.

"Don't try to be funny Emma, I'm not in the mood I've
had a very long day." Admittedly Benjamin did look tired but
unfortunately, he had no choice this time.

"I'll feed you first and perhaps this will give you a
second wind. You have no choice tonight, sweetheart, I'm
afraid." I sounded like a women who hadn't had sex for years
and was desperate.

"Fine, but don't expect much foreplay!"

I look back now and it was tough. The pressure on both
partners to have sex on a given day with an objective in mind
as important as conceiving a child, might at first have
resulted in more intense lovemaking but eventually the
novelty wore off, pretty much like most things that are
contrived.

Benjamin couldn't wait for Thursday to come, he was
off the hook for a while or at least until we knew the
outcome.

The next two weeks went by, I thought, slowly. The wait
was agonising, I kept thinking how wonderful it would be if I
was pregnant. I had bought another two books this time on
names for boys and girls and had circled those I liked most. I
had bought them at one of those 'buy two for one' sales.

Life at the office continued as per normal, except that the
directors began to exclude me from certain meetings I would

ordinarily have attended. They also began to invite Mark to more and more client meetings when I should have been the representative not him.

I decided to pull Mark aside and confront him on the issues.

"Mark, I need to know honestly if my decision to turn down the position of Account Executive for Coopers and Co. has hindered my career here?" Mark and I had always had a relatively open working relationship and I was known for my candour.

"Do you want to know the official answer or the unofficial?"

"Both," I said.

"Officially not, but unofficially and between you and me, you always knew it would Emma. That's the way it works in business. The company looks after those who have unwavering priorities."

"I can't believe this! It may be common practice in the company, but it does not make it right. Do you know that I could take the company to court on this?" I knew my legal rights and this could be construed as sexual discrimination.

"Yes. Now let me tell you a secret. I've mentioned it to one other person so please keep this under wraps. Promise?" Mark trusted me. "I'm going to be leaving the company soon, I have a few ventures pending and I need to move on to greener pastures." The company had negotiated with Mark to head up global marketing during the acquisition of his small firm three years prior. He was due a large payout at the end of three years.

"I thought you might Mark, so it does not come as a shock." Too many chiefs spoil the broth. "Would you advise I take this up with the managing director, Mark?"

"You can, but he's not going to be of much help I don't believe. He called me up when you had said no to the position and asked if I thought you were as good as everyone had said you were in the first place, and if he should be concerned about your commitment going forward." Our MD lived in the United States so I had had little interaction with him.

"What did you say?" I asked.

"I said that you were key talent in the company and just because you declined to take up the position of Account Executive didn't mean you were not committed to the company and amongst those who would help take it forward."

"Thanks. Since when did it become a criminal offence to be a woman and to want both a family as well as a career?" We left the conversation there as Mark's assistant popped her head round the corner to remind him of his next meeting and my question did not require a response it was more of a statement.

I would leave this for now and talk to Benjamin. Perhaps I needed to lay low until I knew what the outcome of the first fertility treatment was.

The two weeks had passed since ovulation induction and I woke the morning I had to take the pregnancy test and threw up three times in the bathroom. I wondered if this was just nerves or if this could be morning sickness. I prayed it was the latter.

Benjamin was already at work, it was Friday and the sun was shining.

I stood up from the floor, washed my face, brushed my teeth, opened the bathroom cupboard and removed the home pregnancy test kit.

I took the test, urinating all over my fingers too. How the hell did one avoid that? Then without looking, left it lying on the top of the toilet seat for about six minutes. I then walked quietly back into the bathroom picked up the tester and looked. I did not believe the result so took out another tester kit; again the result was the same. After three tries, all results being identical I knew the kit wasn't lying. I felt as if I had been hit by a ton of bricks.

I wasn't pregnant.

"May I speak to Benjamin Hogan, please?" I said to the switchboard operator at Benjamin's office.

"Hi darling, this is a pleasant surprise. What's up?" I had told Benjamin I was to take the test the following day so that he wouldn't be distracted at work.

"I…I…oh darling…" I kept bursting into tears unable to get the words out.

"What's the matter Emma?" Benjamin asked anxiously.

"I'm not pregnant." There I had said the words.

"Emma, do you want me to meet you for lunch today?"

"Yes please, I think I might work from home today I don't have any client meetings. I'm not up to going in." In my state it would be better to avoid the office as they would know something was wrong.

"Emma, remember we have each other and we knew it may take more than one attempt. Stay calm, in the meantime why don't you call Phoebe?" Benjamin knew Phoebe would help to calm me as I couldn't turn to Mum, she knew nothing, and I wanted to keep it that way for now. And as for Aunt Viv, she had become increasingly absent-minded of late and it was difficult to communicate. Benjamin and I arranged where to meet for lunch and I replaced the receiver. I never gave Benjamin's emotions another thought until that evening when he came home. I was all consumed by my own feelings.

"Phoebe, I need to chat, have you got five minutes?" Phoebe was at home that day with her twins.

"Absolutely, what's wrong Emma?"

"I found out today that I'm not pregnant. I feel like I have just written my A Levels and failed."

"Did they suggest why it might not have worked?" Phoebe was being practical.

"No, I haven't told them yet."

"Well, I'd call them straight away and tell Dr Collins, ask her why she might think it failed this time. Once you've digested and come to terms with this Emma, you need to pick yourself up and try again; you've only tried once. I fell

72

pregnant second time round. There are many couples out there who've been trying IVF for years and haven't given up."

"Yes I know, but I'm not sure I can go through this again and who knows if it will work second time round. It took ages for the Menopur to take effect and I'm not sure I can cope with the daily suspense." I was full of doubt and uncertainty.

"At least they know now what dosage seems to trigger the growth of the follicles, that's one major step forward and this in itself Emma, would speed up the process next time round. Don't forget why you're doing this. The goal is to conceive, are you still wanting a baby?" Phoebe's question suddenly put things into perspective. I had lost sight of why I was putting my body, heart and mind and Benjamin's mind for that matter, through this ordeal. And it was an ordeal.

"Yes, I can't imagine my life without a child. I've always wanted to be a mother and never doubted that I'd have children. It's just how long is a piece of string?"

"Well, there's your answer then. Hang in there, have faith in Dr Collins and go with the flow. It doesn't matter how long the piece of string is if it's going to get you where you want to go. This is something you cannot control. I know it's hard, but learn to let go a little Em."

My next call was to Dr Collins who wasn't available, so I left a message at reception for her as well as on her mobile phone. I hardly managed to get any work done before noon.

By the time I left our apartment to meet Benjamin for lunch it felt like ten o'clock at night and I had a splitting headache.

"Darling." Benjamin kissed me from across the table in the restaurant, Paula's, on Cheapside. "Did you speak to Phoebe, are you feeling any better?"

"Yes and no, not really."

"What did Dr Collins say?" Benjamin asked.

"I haven't managed to speak to her yet, I've left two messages," I replied.

"Let's wait until you've had a chat with her and go from there. I'm happy to try again or to wait if that's what you decide. Are you free after work tonight or did you plan to go to the gym?" Benjamin asked.

"No, I'm too bushed to go to the gym. Why?"

"Oh, you remember the apartment, Kensington Green, that we liked and put in an offer for?"

"Yes of course the three-bedroom apartment with underground parking in the gated complex with a gym and heated pool." It was my favourite how could I forget.

"The owners have got back to the estate agent and said they'd consider the offer if we upped it by fifty thousand pounds, so I've arranged for us to meet the estate agent there later tonight and have another look at it," Benjamin said.

Benjamin and I had just finished a tour around the three-bedroom apartment in Kensington Green, when my mobile phone started ringing.

"Excuse me," I said to Benjamin and the estate agent and walked out into the foyer.

"Hello, it's Emma Hogan."

"Mrs Hogan, Dr Collins here." Oh, she'd taken me by complete surprise, I needed to get somewhere more private, out of earshot.

"Could I phone you back in five minutes?" I asked.

"Yes, please call back on my mobile phone, I'm not at the unit," Dr Collins said.

"Benjamin, I need to call Dr Collins back. Would you excuse me I'll be outside in the gardens. Could you finish up with Tom?" Tom was the estate agent showing us around the property.

"Sure, chin up," Benjamin said.

I walked outside the building and found a quiet spot on a bench in the communal gardens.

"Dr Collins, so sorry my husband and I are viewing a property and I couldn't talk."

"No problem. I'm returning your call."

"I took the home pregnancy test this morning as you instructed and I'm not pregnant. I'm devastated!"

"Oh, I'm so sorry." That was all she said at first. Then she went on to add, "What do you want to do?"

"Well, that's why I'm calling you really," I said.

"I'm in doubt as to whether I can cope with the disappointment if the second attempt fails. So I'm not sure if I should go down that route again. What are my chances of a successful outcome, the first having failed?"

"I can only advise you to do what your heart is telling you. It is not uncommon for the first attempt to fail; it is not an indication of the outcome of a second attempt. We recommend three attempts using gonatrophins and after that it's IVF. The decision lies with you. Perhaps you and Mr Hogan should talk this over, you may call me anytime to let me know your decision," Dr Collins said calmly.

"I'll talk to Benjamin and get back to you shortly if I may?" My voice sounded weary. All these decisions were taking their toll.

"Yes certainly, think things through." Dr Collins ended the call.

Benjamin and Tom were now standing outside the apartment behind me in the gardens talking. I walked over to them and tried to put on a brave face.

"Emma, I've said to Tom that we'd get back to him once we'd discussed the apartment again together, having now seen it for the third time." After my conversation with Dr Collins I did not really care what happened with the apartment, it seemed now such a trivial matter. We could live in a tiny apartment for the rest of our lives. I wasn't destined to have children anyway.

"So, what did Dr Collins say?" Benjamin asked as we walked back to our apartment on the other side of Kensington High Street.

"Not much, only that we should talk it through and that one failed attempt didn't necessarily mean the second would also fail."

"Didn't she give you her opinion?" Benjamin was clearly confused about what I had actually spoken to her about and why I had called her in the first place if I had no further recommendation as what to do.

"Well, I don't think they're allowed to suggest what they would do, it could make them vulnerable legally if things went pear shaped having followed their advice." I wasn't used to this, back home my doctors always offered their opinion on a matter and left it up to me to decide either way.

"So it's down to you and I then Emma, as it has always been. What's your heart telling you to do?"

"I don't know anymore. I dream of being a mother and having our child, but I dread another disappointment and don't know if I could cope with the reality if I was told it wasn't ever going to be. Perhaps I'd rather not know with such certainty." I was all over the show, my mind was flitting from one view to another and I could not seem to make a decision.

"You're usually so decisive Emma, what's gotten into you lately?" One thing Benjamin loved about me and I knew it, was my independence and self-assuredness.

"I don't know darling, I'm finding it very difficult to make a decision about anything lately. This one's different to any other decision I've had to make before, there's no clear right or wrong." It's easy to make a decision when things are black and white but in this instance everything seemed grey and all I knew was that I wanted to be a mother someday, but I was fighting with the fact that I couldn't understand why it was going to be so hard for me to conceive.

"We can either try again because we want a child sooner rather than later, or we can leave it a while and see if Mother

Nature kicks in and is kind to us, or we can try fertility again in a couple of months. What do you think?"

"I don't mind Emma, it's your decision." Oh drat! For the first time in my life all I wanted was for someone to make the decision for me. "Sleep on it Emma, let your emotions subside and then the answer will become clear." Sadly I've always been a person of instant gratification and I wasn't good at waiting for anything.

I called Dr Collins first thing the next morning; I couldn't wait to tell her my decision, almost as if it might be too late if I left it until the afternoon to call her.

"I must first apologise for calling you on a Saturday but knew you were on call at the Unit today. I wanted to let you know that I've decided to try again. How soon can we start?" I said hastily.

"Oh that's good news, I thought after our telephone call that you didn't have the energy to try again and the disappointment was too great. I'm pleased, since we don't know what your cycle is we can begin straight away."

"When shall I come in?"

"I need to know a few things first Mrs Hogan if I may?" Dr Collins sounded hesitant.

"Sure." I could not think what these could be.

"Are you still running so often?"

"Yes, about five to six times a week, why?"

"Well, I would strongly advise you cut back on the running and slow down a little. I believe your amenorrhoea could be weight related. Your body needs to prepare for pregnancy and the continual pounding running causes, is not ideal while trying to fall pregnant." This was a tall ask, I loved my running. I had done it all my life why must I give up now?

"Do I have to give up altogether?" I asked in disbelief.

"Not all together but I would recommend you take up something less high impact like yoga which you can do throughout pregnancy."

"I'll try." What the heck, it would be just another compromise anyway.

"Let's start a second cycle next week then. I think we'll also give you medication to help thicken the lining so it's more hospitable to your husband's semen."

"Thank you Dr Collins."

We began the process again the following week, starting with a low dose of gonatrophins, but not as low as the first cycle. Dr Collins, worried that my body was now getting used to the process and might respond quicker at a lower dose than before, wanted to be more conservative for fear of multiple embryos.

Meanwhile I was becoming increasingly frustrated at work. Mark was great but never around. He, I was convinced, had begun working on other things quietly in the background ahead of his announcement to the company. Along with his lack of involvement in issues and areas where ordinarily he and I would act as a team, my dedication and passion began to dwindle. The company underwent yet another restructure in an effort to reduce costs internally and to better align them to the new business model. An approach which simply shifted existing problems by moving existing incompetent management around into new positions, rather than replacing them and getting in fresh and experienced leadership.

Somehow, I had resigned myself to the fact that my priorities were shifting.

This time, it only took two weeks for the follicles to respond.

"Mrs Hogan it's good news, look." I leaned over the edge of the examination table almost falling off it when I saw, not one not two but three decent sized follicles on the screen.

"Wow, there're so many!" I exclaimed. It looked like a fish hatchery.

"Well, they're not all the same size, one is clearly larger than the others, it measures 23mm while the other two are smaller at 17mm and 19mm. If you are comfortable we could go ahead and induce ovulation today," Dr Collins said.

"What are the chances of more than one egg being fertilised?" I was thrilled with the outcome but apprehensive of multiple embryos.

"Mrs Hogan the chances are very slight and in your case I would say quite remote." Dr Collins did not hesitate with her response.

"I'll have to call Benjamin if I may before I make the decision." Benjamin would need to know the risks before I went ahead – if I did.

"Sure, you can get dressed now and call from outside the unit. Once you've spoken to Mr Hogan let us know and we'll go from there. You may need to wait a half hour if it's today."

I suppose looking back now, if this hadn't been my first child, I might have made a different decision. But I so desperately wanted a baby.

"Hi. Have you two minutes I'm calling from the hospital?" I asked.

"Hang on let me walk over to the other end of the room for a moment." I heard Benjamin ask his colleague to watch the desk for a moment while he took the call. "OK, you'll have to be quick," he insisted.

"I've got good news, there are three large follicles, one is far larger than the other two, which indicates a healthy egg. Dr Collins has advised that we could go ahead with ovulation induction today if we wish. There is a slight risk that all three may be fertilised, but Dr Collins has assured me that the chances are slim."

"Are you sure about that?" Benjamin sounded a little unsure.

"Yes."

"Then I'd say go ahead," Benjamin responded. "Oh and darling, well done!"

I left the hospital with a sore bum and a smile on my face that stretched from ear to ear.

"I've got a surprise for you, Emma," Benjamin said as he opened the apartment door.

"What sort of surprise?" I said as he slipped an envelope into my hand. I opened it and found two business class seats to Edinburgh for the fifth September.

"Wow, this is exciting. When did you decide to book? Dad will be delighted that we're joining him." Benjamin adored golf, but since we had moved to the United Kingdom he had seldom an opportunity to play.

"I thought we could join him at St Andrews and play some golf for four days and then drive to Fort William. I've found a castle which has been restored as an exclusive lodge where we can base ourselves for five days and do day trips from there." It sounded fantastic just what I think we both needed, something to look forward to.

"Have you told Dad yet?"

"No, thought you could give him the good news yourself," Benjamin said.

"I'll call him later then," I said.

Benjamin and I had always wanted to visit Scotland and this would be a good distraction for us both. My father, an avid golfer spent three weeks at St Andrews each year for the Autumn Meeting as they called it. He went on his own as my mother, who did not play golf, also loathed the drinking and many pub evenings that typically accompanied these few weeks in St Andrews with the members of the Royal and Ancient.

Poor Benjamin, he was on call for the next three days, under pressure to perform once again. There would be no time for sexual spontaneity only time for precision!

"I wonder if every man feels like I do?" Benjamin asked after we had made love one evening after dinner.

"Like how?" I asked.

"Like an instrument that belongs to someone else, your spouse. You have no control as to when you are played and when you are tossed aside." Benjamin, usually the dominant partner had to get used to me taking the initiative for the time being. As it turned out he never quite adjusted to the idea. I, on the other hand, quite enjoyed the change in roles.

"Life as we knew it is gone forever, I'm afraid." I answered as honestly as I could, as much as I would have liked to soothe him and tell him our controlled and perfect life was simply put on hold and we would return to that state of nirvana, I couldn't as he too knew I would be lying.

"Emma?" Benjamin suddenly whispered in the dark of our bedroom.

"Yes, you sound like I should expect a confession." Whenever Benjamin spoke my name as a question I knew something was troubling him.

"I'm not sure how to break this to you, so I've been putting it off for a few days. Basically I need to travel to the States next week again and two weeks after that I'm needed in Geneva." Benjamin quickly followed his first statement with an attempt to prevent my overreacting. "Don't react Emma, it'll be fine, let's think through the fertility schedule and see if this presents a problem."

"Oh Benjamin you promised," I said disappointedly.

"I know and Emma you might have lost track of time, but I've cancelled and postponed trips for the past six weeks already. Pressure is mounting, there are deals going down which I need to be involved in sweetheart," Benjamin said in as calming a voice as possible.

"I know, I can't help it if my body keeps failing me, can I?" I said defensively the tears running down my cheeks. "Funny how we women spend the majority of our young womanhood trying desperately not to fall pregnant and in our prime, wishing we could."

Benjamin pulled me towards him. I fought a little trying to feel sorry for myself and eventually gave in and snuggled up close to his body, my head on his chest as he rubbed my back and held me close in his embrace.

"Let's pray that someone is watching over us and will be kind to us this time." Benjamin kissed my forehead as I tried to stay level headed and reasonable.

Chapter Six

The two-week wait between cycles is perhaps one of the most agonising periods any woman trying to conceive or praying she's not pregnant for that matter, needs to cope with. My mind, like a yo-yo, couldn't keep still. I had to remain busy at work, go for walks everyday, talk to my girlfriends about anything other than childbirth and motherhood and try not to read the little collection of pregnancy books I had accumulated by this time.

I was also getting frustrated and having to come to terms with not running, as Dr Collins had advised. This for someone like me, used to high impact exercise on a regular basis was like smoking thirty cigarettes a day and having to stop overnight, replacing the cigarettes with Nicorettes. It wasn't quite the same sense of satisfaction.

I went into the bathroom, taking the telephone with me. I opened the bathroom cupboard and reached for the home pregnancy test kit once again, only this time I had prepared myself for a negative outcome, as much as I, deep down, had wished for a positive one.

I opened the packaging and pulled out the tester, decided it was all too much and I needed a drink of cold water from the fridge. I couldn't help procrastinating, perhaps in some way I thought this would help dampen my disappointment if the test came back negative.

Benjamin was at work and aware that I was taking the test today, so unlike the time before he was prepared for the worst.

I took the test, careful this time not to urinate on my fingers!

I didn't dare look at the tester and placed it on top of the sceptic tank for five minutes and walked out of the bathroom to put my glass back in the kitchen. I glanced at my watch, five minutes had passed, and that was long enough.

I took one look at the tester and my legs began to quiver, my head began to spin and I suddenly felt weak. Without thinking I lent down again to look at the result and picked the tester up off of the sceptic tank. As I lifted up my head, bang, I hit the cupboard door which I had left ajar, and fell to the floor.

Birds now singing around my ears, my head spinning and my legs quivering, I lay on the floor slumped up against the bathroom wall sobbing my heart out.

There on the floor lay the tester, two unmistakably clear blue lines. I was pregnant!

"May I speak to Benjamin?" I asked one of Benjamin's colleagues who answered the phone.

"Sure, how are you Emma?" Most of Benjamin's colleagues knew me at least by voice if not personally. After all, I was the frantic wife who called regularly.

"Terrific!" I exclaimed bursting with inexplicable joy.

"Hi darling, I know why you're calling. Just say yes or no." Benjamin sounded tense.

"Yes, yes and yes!" I shouted laughing and crying at the same time.

"Emma, I can't believe it. I'm walking into a private meeting room. Hang on a minute." Benjamin's voice was quivering. "Are you absolutely and unmistakably sure?" Benjamin asked.

"Yes, positive, I've taken the test twice," I replied.

"Oh sweetheart that's a miracle." Benjamin was crying, but quietly. "What happens next?" he asked.

"I need to call the hospital and make an appointment. They will take a blood test to confirm the home pregnancy result," I said.

"Let's wait for confirmation, but would you like to go out for supper tonight?" Benjamin sounded relieved.

"Sure. It's such stunning weather why not grab a bite near the park?" We often ate at a restaurant near Kensington Park in summer and being the end of June, the evenings were light until nine o'clock.

I called the hospital and made an appointment for late that afternoon after work.

I arrived at work just after eight o'clock and felt as if I was walking on clouds.

"Emma, what's up you haven't stopped smiling all day?" Mark was suspicious.

"Everything's fine, just having a good day. They are rare nowadays!" I answered not wanting to give anything away.

I arrived at the hospital and was greeted by Dr Collins, which was unusual. I assumed the nursing staff had contacted her and told her the good news.

"Mrs Hogan, congratulations!" Dr Collins walked out of her office towards me as I stood at the reception desk, and shook my hand.

"Thank you, I still haven't fully absorbed the news yet. I'm numb yet exhilarated," I said as I shook her hand. As I said this Lucy walked out and congratulated me also. I felt like these people had become part of my extended family, all of whom appeared almost as ecstatic to see a positive result as Benjamin and I. It was not surprising, as I had seen them at least three times a week for the past twelve weeks.

"Mrs Hogan, we will need to do a blood test to confirm your pregnancy and a vaginal swab, once this has been done we will then do a pelvic ultrasound scan to rule out a multiple pregnancy and check that it is an intrauterine pregnancy. We will not do the ultrasound today, this we will do in ten days time." Dr Collins seemed really pleased for me. I knew she had thought I wouldn't persevere with the treatment after the first attempt failed.

"You've done well Mrs Hogan. Now is the beginning of the next leg of your journey," she said smiling.

"I'm relieved too Dr Collins. I hit an all time low at one point and if it wasn't for my husband I don't believe I would have continued," I said.

"Yes I'm sure. It is the strength of those around and near to us that keep us going sometimes," Dr Collins said with empathy. "I expect to hear the results of the blood tests in two days. One of my staff will contact you. I am also going to prescribe Progesterone for the first twelve weeks of pregnancy to help retain it. These are to be taken in the form of a suppository. Do you know how they work?" Dr Collins asked.

"No, I've never used a suppository before," I answered, only familiar with things like tampons of course.

"Well, they are a medical preparation, bullet-shaped and designed to be placed in your rectum to dissolve and be absorbed into the blood stream. You will need to use one each day for the first twelve weeks of pregnancy," Dr Collins was saying.

Ordinarily I would have squirmed at the thought of placing a suppository in my bottom everyday, but to my surprise I didn't flinch at the thought. I suppose I had been prodded and probed in every other orifice since the start of fertility treatment that this was the only one remaining. It was therefore to be expected that it wouldn't remain virginal for much longer!

"Oh, just be warned Mrs Hogan, the suppositories are quite greasy," Dr Collins added, and left the room while I wondered why this comment was so important.

Benjamin and I ate dinner that evening in a quiet Italian restaurant in Knightsbridge, having walked across Hyde Park from our apartment to get there. It was a beautiful, clear night and the air as fresh as if it had just rained. We sat at our table talking over the day's events and planning our future now we had been blessed with a child growing inside me. I felt untouchable. I felt like the luckiest person alive.

We spoke of what type of apartment we needed with a small child in London and if the one at Kensington Green was still our favourite. We chatted about names and if we wanted to find out the gender. We also spoke about who and when we'd tell our families about the news.

"Benjamin I don't want to tell anyone until I am past the twelve week mark. It has taken me so long to fall pregnant that I'd feel an idiot, a failure, if I told everyone and then lost the baby." I was adamant I wanted no one to know, not even Aunt Viv who sadly wouldn't remember even if I did.

"If that's what you want then that's what we'll do Emma. It will be hard though and you cannot tell anyone else, word travels quickly and if you do, word will get out," Benjamin said.

"Yes I know, I'll tell no one," I promised. "It's ironic but looking at the dates, I'll be twelve weeks pregnant during the time we're in Scotland with Dad."

"Wow, I hadn't looked that far ahead but you're right. Funny that!" Benjamin remarked. "Golf and champagne, couldn't think of a better combination!"

The blood tests came back positive, confirming the home pregnancy test result, while the swab came back negative, all clear.

"Emma, you're needed in South Africa for a two day strategy session." It was Mark standing over me at my desk and I hadn't noticed until then.

"When?" I asked, now conscious of the fact that I was pregnant and should I even fly.

"Next week. Thought you and I could stay on to discuss the budget with our MD while we're there. He'll be out for a couple of days from New York. It'll be a five day trip," Mark said.

I calculated the days in my head while I sat there and worked out that this would coincide with the day of my scan to rule out a multiple pregnancy. I had to think quickly without giving my state away.

"I think Benjamin and I have house guests for part of the time," I lied, "perhaps we could stay on just for a day and cut the trip short by two days?"

"It'll be back to back meetings then all day, no time to play?" Mark loved South Africa for its magnificent wildlife. He had obviously thought he'd stay an extra day at the Safari Lodge where the strategy session was taking place, to talk and meet with the other directors. Tough, I had more important priorities right now. "Well, I might stay on then for that extra time, but I'll get Janet to set up the meetings for us and to make sure they all take place the day after the strategy session before everyone leaves the Lodge." Janet was Mark's PA.

Phew, I thought, I got off that one lightly.

I had just enough time to see Aunt Viv while I was in South Africa. Mum had told me how she had deteriorated but nothing prepared me for the shock of seeing her. It was as if life had been sucked out of her. Pale and terribly thin, she stayed indoors now and seldom ventured beyond the boundaries of her room.

"Aunt Viv, I've brought you a surprise," I said, trying to disguise my disbelief by sounding chipper.

"Oh, Judy so good of you to come and see me," Viv said.

"No Viv, it's me, Emma-Beez," I said kissing her gently on both cheeks.

"But Emma's not here, she ran away a long time ago." Viv was confused. At least she knew I hadn't been in South Africa for a while.

"Well, she's back especially to see you and look what she's carrying," I said as I pointed to my tummy.

"Have you seen Bobby?" Viv asked lost in a world of her own making.

"No, I haven't but he did send a message. He said to tell you he thinks of you often and you're still his special girl." I played along realising it wasn't any good telling Viv in secret what was going on. She'd not understand and if she did she would tell someone during one of her monologues. I spent two hours with her and then as I got up to leave to my amazement she took my hand in hers and spoke as if she'd been engaged in the conversation all along.

"Emma-Beez, I'm losing my mind. I can't seem to control what's happening to me. I'm frightened. Please help me to go peacefully now, I'm ready to join Bobby." Viv squeezed my hand and then let go, a tear trickled down her left cheek as I wiped it with my finger.

My throat tightened as I swallowed the tears, my dearest beloved aunt was suffering. It was then that I knew, now that she'd seen me, it wouldn't be long before she'd let go of this world and fulfil her dreams by joining Bobby.

I flew back from South Africa feeling jaded, exhausted and hung-over although I hadn't drunk and wasn't allowed to drink a single drop of alcohol. I had never been so tired before. My body felt as if it had been drugged. What was worse I had horrendous morning sickness, which hit me like a ton of bricks on the flight home.

"Hello weary traveller. How was the flight?" Benjamin asked when he collected me from Paddington Station.

"Besides having to throw up five times during the night, fine I suppose. Fortunately Mark wasn't flying back with me, he'd have guessed," I said. "I'm famished, not surprising seeing everything I ate just came straight back up."

"I've missed you." Benjamin kissed me three times. "Let's get you home, shower up and we can then have breakfast at Starbucks. How's that sound?" Benjamin sensed my weariness.

"Sounds good to me." I had arranged to fly back on the Friday flight so I could be home for the weekend. Mark stayed on and was flying back on Sunday night.

"Did you take it easy?" Benjamin sounded concerned for my well-being.

"Yes I did, chose to skip the early morning game drives before the strategy session began and only went on the night drives. It was freezing." I had forgotten how cold the nights could get in South Africa during those few midwinter months.

I showered immediately we arrived home and dressed in a cool skirt and blouse before downing a cold glass of water and grabbing a banana on the way out.

"What did you eat while I was away?" I asked Benjamin, as I had noticed of all the things I had bought before going on my trip all that seemed eaten were the pizzas.

"Oh, I see you've been checking up on me already," Benjamin responded.

"You're going to get scurvy," I noted as I closed the fridge come freezer door.

"You're right. No time to prepare, so I indulged in my favourite." Benjamin loved pizza and whenever I was out of town he seized the opportunity to overdose on them.

We had a delicious breakfast and caught up on each other's news. Benjamin was concerned about my work as always and wanted to know if this would be one of many trips while I was pregnant. I hadn't given it much thought until now, but he was right, something I'd have to work out before approaching Mark. There wasn't much I could do until I officially told Mark that I was pregnant, which wouldn't be for another month. It would have to wait until I got back from Scotland.

"Benjamin?" I asked.

"Yes," Benjamin said.

"Would you come with me this time for my first scan to see the embryo, it's on Monday this week?" I asked him.

Up until then I hadn't put any pressure on Benjamin to join me, unlike most other women in the unit who I always saw together with their husbands. Of course it wasn't always the woman that had the fertility problems.

"Sure, I'm glad you asked as I was going to ask you myself. Wouldn't miss the first viewing of our child to be," Benjamin said excitedly.

Benjamin and I sat quietly in the waiting room at the hospital late on Monday afternoon. My hands felt clammy and I apologised to Benjamin who was holding one.

"Mrs Hogan would you like to come through please?" It was Lucy.

"Lucy this is my husband Benjamin Hogan. He'll be joining me in the examination room today if that's possible?"

"No problem. Good to meet you Mr Hogan, we'd began to wonder if you actually existed," Lucy said jokingly. "Just wait in here while Dr Collins joins you," Lucy instructed.

I undressed as usual in the consultation room, climbed up onto the examination table and asked Benjamin to pass me a clean white sheet.

"Glad you're covering up," Benjamin said, "I thought for a moment you weren't going to."

"Once you've seen one naked woman you've seen them all I suppose, darling," and with that Dr Collins walked into the room.

"Hello Mrs Hogan good to see you again. I assume this is Mr Hogan?" Dr Collins asked.

"Yes, please meet my husband Benjamin. Hope it's alright if he joins me for the scan today?"

"Glad you could come. The first scan is such a special one it is wonderful when both partners can experience it together," Dr Collins said as she prepared the probe and condom, which she slid as usual over it. "Let's take a look."

I was tense with apprehension. Not knowing what I was going to see unnerved me somewhat. I had never seen an embryo on a scan before. Dr Collins turned the screen towards me and, as I looked first at her face and then at Benjamin's, I knew there was something wrong. My heart fell and I began to tremble.

"What's the matter you look as if you've seen a ghost Benjamin? Dr Collins I cannot see the image properly from this angle." My neck was in agony, I had twisted it so far around it almost fell off.

"Nothing to worry about Mrs Hogan. It is great news, here you go. Let me explain the image to you and what you are looking at." With that Dr Collins moved the trolley with the scanner on top right around so I could clearly see the entire image.

Even I could understand the image to know there was not one but two embryos growing inside me. I wasn't sure now what to think, how to react; should I be over the moon, which I was, or should I be panic stricken, which I was also? How could I carry two babies with my small frame? Twins always come early; I didn't want premature babies and all the problems associated with them. Would I manage to continue working with two? Could we afford two children? What kind of help would I need? All these questions popped into my head and it began to spin. Benjamin sensed my concerns and took my hand in his, squeezing it gently, smiling at me for reassurance.

"Darling it's a miracle! They look like little tadpoles!" Benjamin exclaimed.

"Mrs Hogan as you have already guessed you are carrying two embryos. Here's the one heartbeat and here on this side is the other. You're pregnant with twins," Dr Collins confirmed. I felt stunned. "It is wonderful news," she added.

"Dr Collins, how am I going to carry two babies? I don't think I'm big enough, my uterus won't stretch that far," I remarked.

"You'll be absolutely fine, don't panic. It is early days, sometimes one embryo is absorbed back into the body and only one continues to grow. We need to wait and see," Dr Collins cautioned.

"I thought you said it was highly unlikely that more than one would be fertilised when we decided to go ahead with ovulation induction?" I said.

"Yes and it is unusual that you have two eggs fertilised, the chances of this were slim, but they did exist which we made clear at the start," Dr Collins said gently.

"Perhaps I'm just overwhelmed right now. I need a little time to adjust to the news," I said, as I lay back on the examination table to clear my head.

"Darling, I'm so excited, we're going to have two. I'm so proud of you," Benjamin said. He was amazing; always there to support me and provide me with reassurance and strength, nothing seemed too great for him to handle. He wasn't going to let on even if he was as shocked as I was.

I slowly began thinking through the reality of what was happening to me, to us, and as my mind filtered the information and digested it, so my heart began to beat faster until I too overcame the initial shock and all I felt was jubilation. It became clear to me that this was what was meant to be.

"Sweetheart, not only do you have swimmers but they swim excellent freestyle!" I said jokingly as we left the hospital arm in arm.

I had heard about morning sickness but never realised how absolutely rotten you feel. It hit me like a tornado and I was only ten weeks pregnant. I felt as if I had a permanent hangover only without the fun that goes with partying the nights away! I felt so awful it became increasingly difficult for me to sit through a meal out with friends, to sit still for very long at work or to hold a client meeting. I kept running to the bathroom every half hour making all sorts of excuses. I could keep very little down. I had rung Dr Collins and she had explained that it is often worse with multiples.

"Benjamin?" I asked, as we were getting ready for a wedding we were going to that afternoon.

"Yes, what's up?" Benjamin replied trying to get his cufflinks through the holes in his shirt. I walked over to where he was standing and as I helped him with his cufflinks I continued. "I'm worried about my current condition; I'm going to be running to the toilet every couple of minutes. Someone at the wedding is bound to guess what's going on."

"I wouldn't worry, you don't usually drink alcohol so that won't be any different and as far as the toilet thing goes we can say you've had a stomach bug and you are just getting over it," Benjamin said.

I had intended to wear a rusty red dress, one of my favourites and one I always felt good in, but when I came to zip the back up I found that my stomach had grown and the bloody zip wouldn't close. Oh hell! I had to think quickly and try to see which of the other black tie dresses in my wardrobe would fit.

"Oh drat Benjamin you won't guess but my zip won't close. What am I going to wear?" I shouted.

"Relax, you can always wear a jacket on top and leave the zip half undone!" Benjamin tried to be humorous.

"I don't have time for your jokes. We'll be late," I retorted.

I finally found something I could wear but for safety I took a pashmina with me as a wrap around, afraid this dress might pop. I seemed to be expanding hourly!

We arrived at the wedding a minute late, fortunately for us the bride was running late as usual. Why is it a bride always runs late on her wedding day?

"Hi Benjamin, hi Emma. Running a little late!" John and Susan said as we sat down next to them in the pew in a little church in East Horsley.

"Yes as usual all Emma's fault," Benjamin said jokingly.

"Susan you look great how far along are you now?" I asked.

"I'm twenty-nine weeks already, time flies," Susan said.

"Have you found out the gender yet?" I asked.

"Yes, we're expecting a little girl,' Susan said.

"And the doctors better be right otherwise we'll be dressing our son in pink!" John interjected. Susan had apparently a wardrobe full of pink girl's clothes already. "It'll be an expensive mistake if they're wrong," John added.

"When are you two going to start?" Bianca asked.

Bianca and Ross were close friends of ours who had been living in London for over six years.

"Soon, but not yet, we've only just moved to the UK," I lied. Benjamin and I had rehearsed what we'd say to anyone who asked so our stories were consistent.

The ceremony finished and I, having needed to slip out during it, jumped up as soon as the bride and groom, Sophie and Steve, and the bridal party had exited the church, ran for the nearest toilets.

I had brought a suppository with me, as I had to take one twice daily, so after being sick yet again and administering the suppository I felt quite unattractive, certainly not in the mood for an all night party. I looked in the mirror as I put on my lipstick and brushed my hair and thought quietly to myself: you've dreamed of this and now you've got what you asked for so don't complain.

"How are you feeling?" Benjamin asked as we drove in convoy to the reception.

"Not great, but I'll be alright as long as I can slip out whenever I need to without being noticed. Perhaps we can rearrange the seating plan at our table so I am nearest the exit?" I asked Benjamin.

"Sweetheart let's see, I'm sure it will be a marquee and we'll be able to move freely in and out. There are so many people at the wedding that they won't even notice. Relax, won't you please?" Benjamin said, having clearly had enough of all the fuss.

The wedding reception took place at Steve's parents' home in East Horsley, a beautiful and quaint village in Surrey. As we drove up the long gravel driveway I remarked how picturesque the setting was. Tall oaks flanked the driveway, which must have been at least fifty years old.

Beneath which Steve's mother, an ardent gardener, had planted a mass of lilac and white crocuses. To the left of the driveway was a paddock in which three horses: a chestnut and two greys were grazing. Steve's sister, whose family lived in the cottage on the estate, was an excellent horse rider. As we approached the main house I was taken aback at how perfectly it blended in with the natural surroundings. The house, consistent with a Tudor style, lay tucked away, nestled between a small stream to the east and a set of pine trees to the west. As our party of friends made their way to the pre-dinner drinks marquee where we ordered our drinks and had time to take in the setting, I was suddenly compelled by the idea that we shouldn't be looking in the city for a home after all, we should be looking out in the country. Rambling roses surrounded the house, 'Pink Perpetue' and 'Silver Moon', between which at ground level grew purple lavender and white lilies interspersed with pink geraniums. Everything was in full spring splendour.

We were seated at a table along with ten of our closest friends so we were in familiar company. Benjamin had swapped my place setting with Bianca's so I was nearest the exit. I was so concerned about my vomiting that I hadn't even given the suppository another thought. It was Susan who noticed the greasy mark at the back of my dress near my bottom and it was Susan who pulled me quietly aside after making one of the many trips to the toilet.

"Emma, I need to tell you something," Susan called over to me from the opposite end of the table when I returned from the ladies.

I walked over to Susan and crouched down beside her chair. She lent over and whispered in my ear.

"Emma, you've got a mark on your dress at the back, it's quite large and very visible," Susan said gently. "I noticed it as you were walking away from the table to the toilet."

My disappearing acts hadn't gone unnoticed after all.

"Thanks Susan, can't think what it is, I'll go to the ladies now and see," I said.

"Do you want me to join you?" Susan asked.

"No, no really I'll be fine." I didn't want Susan to join me as she'd surely ask too many prying questions. I picked up my pashmina and quickly scuttled off to the toilet once again.

Thank God for my pashima! Dr Collins had warned me about the suppositories being greasy but I hadn't taken heed. All over the back of my olive green chiffon dress was a grease mark the size of a small football. Obviously after administering the progesterone suppository at the church and having sat in the car some of the medication had leaked out onto my dress! My pashmina would have to be worn for the rest of the evening even on the dance floor! I felt like such an idiot. That was certainly not my best wedding, but it would be one I'd remember for years to come.

My morning sickness continued unremittingly. I was restless at night and found myself getting really tired at work. I had expanded and while no one at work had guessed that I was pregnant, to the unsuspecting eye my figure hadn't changed but to Benjamin and I my waist had expanded. I often found myself lying awake in the middle of the night, just thinking about the children growing inside of me and how my every movement could be felt by both babies. I used to stroke my stomach and gently talk to my unborn children. My world narrowed considerably and its focal point became those two little embryos inside of me. They were all I could think about.

Now towards the end of the first trimester, Dr Collins had referred me to an obstetrician and gynaecologist who would deliver my babies for me. Their job at the Assisted Conception Unit was now technically complete. My first introductory consultation with Dr Geoffrey had gone well and I was due back that week, the start of my twelfth week of pregnancy, for a Nuchal Translucency scan. Knowing at that point very little about this scan, I hadn't given it a second thought.

"Good afternoon may I help you?" the receptionist asked, as I entered the ultrasound waiting rooms in Harley Street.

"Yes, I'm here for my Nuchal Translucency scan with Dr Geoffrey. My name is Mrs Emma Hogan," I said.

"Ah yes. Please take a seat, Dr Geoffrey will be right with you," the receptionist said.

As I sat in the waiting room I paged through the various magazines but was not reading the content. Instead, from behind the pages of the glossy magazines, I tried to estimate how far along each woman in the waiting room was by carefully studying the size of their tummies. It was hard to tell really and if I were anything to go by people would think I was twenty weeks pregnant but, in reality, I was only entering my twelfth week.

The door opened and a lady walked out of Dr Geoffrey's office. At first I did not notice, too caught up in my own thoughts, but at second glance I saw tears running down her cheeks. Dr Geoffrey asked her to wait in the waiting room while his assistant asked her if she would like a glass of water or herbal tea. I wondered then what the matter was.

"Come through Mrs Hogan," Dr Geoffrey said. "How are you today?" he asked, as I climbed up onto the examination table and lifted my blouse for the scan. I felt a cold chill run down my back as he smeared the sticky gel over my tummy. It felt like he'd dumped an entire bucket load of gelatine onto my stomach.

"I'm still suffering from constant nausea, it hasn't let up yet. I had expected it to go by twelve weeks or that was what I was told."

"Mrs Hogan you're carrying twins, most of what people tell you will not ring true for you. It's slightly different carrying two. Let's see how the nausea goes, if it doesn't get better by sixteen weeks and you're unable to keep any food down then we'll have to prescribe some medication. Are you able to keep anything down?" he asked.

"Yes and no. It depends what I eat," I said. "Surprisingly enough, I am able to eat immediately after vomiting, so I think I'm retaining some nutrients."

"Alright, let's keep an eye on this and see," Dr Geoffrey advised. "Now you're aware we are going to do the Nuchal Translucency scan today?" Dr Geoffrey asked.

"Yes," I replied.

"Do you know why we do this scan?" Dr Geoffrey asked.

"No not really. All I know is that it has something to do with detecting Down's Syndrome," I said honestly.

"Yes in part. I'll measure the amount of fluid at the back of each of your babies' necks. We then use this measurement, together with your age and the age of the foetus, to determine the risk associated with the likelihood of your babies having a chromosomal abnormality," Dr Geoffrey said. He obviously saw the concern on my face and added, "No need to worry this is non-invasive and won't harm the foetuses in any way."

As Dr Geoffrey moved the scanner probe over my stomach I could see the little foetuses, my babies, moving peacefully in the amniotic fluid. I could hardly believe how well formed they were already. I could identify their eyes, their feet, their hands and their little hearts beating to their own rhythm.

"Right, Mrs Hogan, I've measured the fluid at the back of foetus one's neck and plotted this on the graph taking into account your age. This foetus appears absolutely normal with a one in three thousand chance of chromosomal abnormality." He paused there for a moment, it seemed like a half hour before he continued when in fact it was only a couple of seconds. My heart fell, it began beating faster and I knew instinctively that something was wrong with the second foetus.

"I had difficulty taking a reading from the second foetus since it moved constantly, but the final reading I took indicates a slightly increased risk of chromosomal abnormality with a one in three hundred and nine chance," Dr Geoffrey said.

Bang! The news hit me like a fatal bullet to the heart, dead centre. There was a high probability that one of the little foetuses I was carrying could be a Down's baby. My mind raced, I swallowed hard the tears welling in my eyes. What did this all mean? There is no family history on either side of abnormalities, was I being punished for having cheated Mother Nature and undergone fertility treatment? Was this her way of getting back at me?

"Mrs Hogan, are you alright?" Dr Geoffrey asked.

"No. I'm not sure what this result means exactly," I said.

"There is no need to panic. All that this result means is that the fluid behind the neck is thicker than usual, which in itself carries a higher risk of chromosomal abnormality. It is not conclusive however," he replied.

I must have looked at him still disbelievingly as he continued by adding:

"I would like to redo the test on the second foetus in twenty minutes, in the hope that the little one has settled down and stopped moving quite so much."

"What if the result doesn't change? Can I find out for certain if there's a real problem?" I asked, devastated by this news.

"I understand that it is difficult to know what to do for the best. Let me explain your options to you," Dr Geoffrey said empathetically. "You can either await events and repeat the scan at nineteen weeks gestation. A normal scan will halve the pre-existing risk to one in six hundred. This has the advantage that it is non-invasive," Dr Geoffrey explained.

"But that is still a higher risk than the risk for foetus one is it not?" I asked.

"Yes," Dr Geoffrey replied. "Your second option is to have an amniocentesis," Dr Geoffrey said.

"What's an amniocentesis?" I asked naively.

"I extract a small amount of amniotic fluid from the amniotic sac using a syringe and this is sent off for chromosome analysis. I'm afraid it is associated with a one percent risk of miscarriage. The advantage of this invasive method is that the results are conclusive," Dr Geoffrey continued.

"What about a blood test? I seem to recall friends of mine had blood tests done," I asked.

"If you were carrying a single foetus we could perform a blood test, but since you are carrying two we would not be able to differentiate between foetuses," Dr Geoffrey said.

"Do I run the risk of losing the other foetus as well, if I opt for an amnio?" I asked.

"Yes, I'm afraid with twins both foetuses are at risk. I will have to take fluid from each sac and will need to penetrate the first in order to get to the second sac," Dr Geoffrey said, with a level of sincerity I've seldom come across.

I wasn't sure just then if I would have preferred to be shielded from the truth.

"These are difficult decisions to make, ones you shouldn't take lightly. Perhaps you should talk these over with Mr Hogan before making a decision. You have until sixteen weeks to make that decision."

"Why so far off?" I asked.

"The amnio must be performed then and cannot be performed before if you want conclusive results," Dr Geoffrey said. "But as I said, I would like to redo the measurement for the second foetus to make sure. Would you like to call your husband from outside the waiting room and I'll take a second measurement in twenty minutes between my other patients?" he asked.

"Yes, I would like that very much," I said.

It suddenly struck me that the lady I had seen crying earlier might have heard bad news. News like my own or worse. She might have heard conclusive news; she might have lost the foetus. There could have been any number of complications that could have arisen. Falling pregnant is hard enough, I never thought staying pregnant and carrying a healthy baby was just as hard.

"Benjamin I'm calling from the ultrasound rooms. Can you chat briefly?" I asked.

"Hang on let me call you back in five minutes," Benjamin replied on the other end of the phone.

I paced the hallway outside the waiting room for five minutes going over and over in my mind first what the news meant, second if I could have prevented this and third what decision I should make. I could not decide and did not want to have to decide.

It wasn't fair, why me, why us, why now after all we'd been through to get here? The black and white checked floor tiles of the hallway felt cold under my feet even though I had shoes on and the walls suddenly started to cave in on me and I felt claustrophobic. I walked quickly out of the building into Harley Street; I needed some fresh air.

The phone rang. "Benjamin, thank goodness for your voice," I said.

"Emma, what's the matter?" Benjamin asked.

Benjamin was out of town on business again and I had called him on his mobile phone.

"I had my nuchal scan today. It's good and bad news. The first foetus is fine, but there is a higher risk of an abnormality with the second." I then broke down.

"Stay calm Emma, take three deep breaths, think clearly," Benjamin instructed and then paused.

"What do you mean by abnormality and what degree of risk, darling?" Benjamin continued.

"By abnormality, Dr Geoffrey means Down's Syndrome, Spina Bifida and the like. The risk is one in three hundred and nine for twin two whereas twin one's risk is one in three thousand," I explained. "Oh Benjamin why me, why us, why now?" I asked, half not expecting an answer.

"What did the doctor say you should do now?" Benjamin asked.

"Nothing except that we have two options. Either we wait until we have the scan repeated at nineteen weeks when, if all is normal, the risk is halved to one in six hundred but there're no guarantees all the same. Or we have an amniocentesis at sixteen weeks, which will give us a conclusive answer," I explained.

"What's the catch?" Benjamin the sceptic asked.

"There's a down side as always. It carries a one percent risk of miscarriage. That's for each baby," I said.

"Do you have to make a decision now? Can't you wait for me to get home tomorrow night so we can talk through this quietly together?" Benjamin asked.

"I don't have to make a decision now but we do by sixteen weeks as this is when the amnio must be done," I stressed to Benjamin. "I don't think I could be a good mother to an abnormal child," I confessed out loud.

"Emma, the reading doesn't mean that the one baby is abnormal it only means it is at a higher risk of being abnormal. Why don't you call Dr Collins and ask her what she would do?" Benjamin said.

"I hadn't thought of that, yes I will later tonight once I'm home from work," I said. "I miss you terribly, I really need you, I'm not coping so well."

"I'll be home tomorrow, darling, and then we have our trip to Scotland to look forward to this coming weekend. We'll be away for ten days, it'll do us good," Benjamin said.

I walked back into the ultrasound waiting rooms. Dr Geoffrey redid the scan but the measurement came back the same and the foetus hadn't moved, so there could be no doubting the accuracy that time.

Chapter Seven

London came alive in springtime. The cherry blossoms were out; the daffodils, tulips and crocuses appear en mass as if from nowhere. Everywhere I looked there were hanging baskets bursting with flowers. Even the usually grey faces of people walking the streets seemed merrier. Only I felt bewildered, lost and all alone. I couldn't help but think over and over that perhaps I was being punished for having had fertility, when I should have accepted my fate and kept trying naturally, trusting in whatever would be would be.

I caught the tube back to work and walked into the office with a somewhat dull and gloomy face.

"Emma, you've finally managed to put some meat on those skinny bones," Harold called out to me from across the open plan office. Harold was one of the board directors out from Asia for three days to meet with one of our partners. If only he knew I thought.

"Indeed, I've been eating chocolates," I said in as joking a voice as I could muster. "How are you?" I asked trying to sound enthusiastic and switch my mind away from the results of the scan.

"Fine, thought you might want to join myself and Allan for our meeting today. Their marketing director will also be there?" Harold asked. Allan Crawford being the global sales director.

"Sure, has it got anything to do with the project I'm already working on with them?" I asked.

"That's part of it but the bigger picture is to build a stronger global tie with them through various initiatives and joint client engagements," Harold said.

"What time and where?" I asked.

"I'll drive, it's at their HQ near Heathrow Airport. We're meeting at five o'clock," Harold said.

Oh drat I'd wanted to call Dr Collins tonight to seek her advice. I'd have to snatch five minutes sometime that afternoon to speak to her before the meeting.

"Fine, I'll give you guys a project update on the way so you're fully in the picture as to what we've been doing with them so far," I said. "Also, just bear in mind I'm off for the next week and a bit, taking some much needed leave and going to Scotland. So won't be able to progress anything until I'm back," I added.

"A vacation is a great time to get work done." Harold I hoped was joking.

Later that afternoon I slipped out of the office to call Dr Collins. I prayed she was going to answer her mobile phone. I needed to hear her opinion.

"Dr Collins, it's Emma Hogan, may I speak to you for a moment?" I asked.

"I'm in the middle of something. Could you call back in five minutes? I'll be done by then," Dr Collins said.

"Sure, I'll call back in five minutes on this number," I replied.

I wondered what Dr Collins would say. I knew she was conservative so I imagined her response would be to do nothing.

"Hi Mrs Hogan, my apologies for not taking your call earlier. I hope all's going well with the pregnancy. What can I do for you?" Dr Collins asked.

"Dr Collins I've just had my nuchal scan and I'm concerned. The first twin's measurement is fine but the second places the foetus at an increased risk of abnormality. I'm not sure what to do," I said.

"How high is the risk?" Dr Collins asked.

"It is a one in three hundred and nine chance," I said.

"Yes, that's quite high. They usually recommend an amnio for any result higher than a one in two hundred chance of abnormality," she said pensively.

"What would you do if you were in my shoes?" I asked.

"You are asking my opinion, which is also subjective just like anyone else's. I'll tell you what I think." She paused for emphasis. "You and your husband have undertaken great lengths to conceive, your parents and those before them did not have the luxury of all the information and technology available nowadays so they would have continued a pregnancy oblivious. I believe that there is too much information, too many tests nowadays which only complicate matters and cause additional stress to the expectant parents, often for no reason." Dr Collins paused again momentarily. "I would do nothing." That was Dr Collins' answer, just as I had expected.

"Thank you. I appreciate your time and your honesty," I said.

"Not a problem, my pleasure. I'd also talk to Dr Geoffrey, in my opinion he's the one who would know best what to do. Good luck," Dr Collins replied.

As a child I always wanted to make my own decisions. I got frustrated every time my parents or my teachers told me what to do. Why then was it, all I wanted now was for someone to make the decision for me?

Meanwhile, our meeting went off smoothly and by the time Harold and Allan dropped me back home it was late. Benjamin had left a message saying he was boarding his plane at the airport and would see me in the morning. We were leaving for Scotland in the afternoon. I couldn't wait. I desperately needed a change of scenery.

I didn't sleep a wink that night and when Benjamin arrived home that afternoon from his business trip the stress was obviously showing in my eyes and on my face.

"Emma, you look finished. I think you need to relax while we're away. Why don't you book a couple of massage and facial appointments while your father and I are out playing golf? I believe the indoor pool is also great for swimming," Benjamin said as he finished unpacking one suitcase only to repack another.

"I'm perplexed. On the one hand I don't truly believe there's anything wrong with our second baby but on the other I know I couldn't raise an abnormal child so I need to know for certain. But the cost of knowing is so high," I said desperately.

"Darling, I think that we should wait until we get back from Scotland to make a decision. The decision will come to us over the next ten days. We'll know what to do for the best. Right now you're way too emotional," Benjamin said, cool and calm as ever. His feathers never seemed to ruffle. While I on the other hand seemed a permanent wreck!

We flew into Edinburgh at six o'clock that evening. It was warm and the air felt fresh and clean – a pleasant change from the polluted air in London. Benjamin had arranged for a hired car, which we collected and then set off for St Andrews. I was delegated the task of navigator, something which I was ordinarily not bad at, but since falling pregnant my sense of direction had vanished. The Avis car rental assistant advised we take the M90 through Kinross and then take the A91 through Cupar to St Andrews rather than taking the A92. It seemed straight forward enough.

We drove over the Forth Road Bridge and as we drove further away from Edinburgh, so the landscape became more rural. I was struck by the profound impression of space, the vastness of open land and the degree of serenity and quiet the landscape portrayed. There had been floods the week prior to our journey and places like Inverness had been closed to tourists. Fortunately we arrived the week of sunshine, which turned out to be the best weather Scotland had had in September for twenty years. Just what we both needed!

The conversation revolved mostly around Benjamin's business trip and our activities for the next ten days. We both avoided the topic of an amniocentesis. As we approached Cupar I asked Benjamin to stop the car.

"What's the matter, darling?" Benjamin asked as he pulled over to the side of the road.

"Nothing serious, just step out of the car and look to your left," I said as we both stepped out of the car.

"Wow, that's awesome!" Benjamin exclaimed as he saw what had caught my eye.

On the horizon to the west was a sight I had never seen and I'm sure may never see again. Two fully formed rainbows whose arcs joined at the horizon were stretched across the evening sky. Their colours so vivid set a contrast against the deep blue sky.

"This is a sign, we're supposed to have two babies," Benjamin whispered in my ear as he kissed my forehead and held me for a moment to take it all in, gently moving his hands over my abdomen.

Surprises of surprises I managed to get us both safely to St Andrews without a single glitch!

"Mr and Mrs Hogan, there's a message for you from a Mr Paul Sutherland." The gentleman behind the check-in desk handed us a handwritten note. It was my father's handwriting.

Welcome to Scotland. I'm playing golf and should be in the informal bar from seven o'clock with the boys. Join me when you get in. I'm expecting you around eight o'clock.

Signed *Dad.*

We both looked at our watches, it was eight fifteen, we'd better hurry I thought.

We didn't bother taking a shower, just brushed our teeth, and I combed my hair and had just enough time to squirt some perfume and put some lipstick on, when Benjamin tugged my arm. We didn't notice the bottle of champagne on the table in our room.

"Your father's been waiting a while let's get moving," Benjamin instructed.

Dad was sitting with two other gentlemen when we walked into the bar. He hadn't seen us so we walked quietly over to where he was sitting.

"Hi Dad, it's so good to see you," I said as he stood up and we embraced each other. I hadn't seen him for three months since my last business trip to South Africa in my early days of pregnancy.

"Hello Beans, hi Benjamin. So you arrived safe and sound. Did you get my note?" he asked. My father had always called me Beans ever since I could remember.

"Hi Paul. Yes, it's an easy journey from Edinburgh. Even your daughter's navigational skills didn't mislead us," Benjamin said jokingly, as he shook my father's hand and Dad nudged him on the shoulder.

"Let me introduce you to two of my golfing colleagues," Dad continued. "Alistair Seals and David Hughes."

"Pleased to meet you," Benjamin and I said at the same time.

"What can I get you two travellers to drink?" my father asked. "Emma, you look terrific, the English cuisine is obviously agreeable!" Dad added as he squeezed my cheeks. I blushed; did I look like a puffer fish? Dad was always in the habit of passing personal comments unintentionally in front of strangers.

"A Scotch on the rocks thanks. Emma will have a lime and soda," Benjamin replied, knowing without having to ask what I'd have.

"Why don't you be a sport Emma and have a gin and tonic?"

"Thanks but no thanks Dad, I think I'll pass out if I have a gin. Lime and soda will do fine for now," I answered as casually as possible. I was not a big drinker so it wasn't that unusual not be drinking alcohol.

"I see the London pubs haven't influenced your drinking habits though," he said as he walked over to the bar counter to order our drinks.

We sat and chatted about their day on the golf course, about our work in London and about St Andrews itself. An hour later Alistair and David said their goodnights as they were joining another party for dinner.

"Have you two had anything to eat?" Dad asked as we finished our last round of drinks. It was ten o'clock and I didn't feel like eating a large dinner. Benjamin had snacked on the flight, but I was sure if I hadn't been around he'd have loved to join the men.

"No, not really, but we're not that hungry," Benjamin said.

"I thought you may not be hungry and that you would want to shower and have an early night. So I arranged to join others for dinner. They started at half past nine, you're more than welcome to join us," Dad said.

I felt relieved that he hadn't planned a special dinner as I was tired and felt nauseas.

"Dad what are your plans tomorrow?" I asked.

"I've booked a time for Benjamin and I to tee off at nine thirty tomorrow morning on the Old Course. You've never played it before have you?" Dad asked.

"No, I've never been to Scotland even, so I'd be delighted to play," Benjamin replied, all excited.

"I've also booked a time for us on Sunday at Carnoustie. That will be an all day outing so Emma you're more than welcome to join us and walk the course. I have booked a table at the best fish restaurant in St Andrews for tomorrow night." Dad had tried for years to get me to play golf and impart his enthusiasm for the game, but with little success. My brothers on the other hand loved their golf and were all single handicaps. Thank goodness Benjamin enjoyed golf. It earned him immediate acceptance by the male members of my family back when we were dating. In fact in South Africa, at times I had felt like a golfing widow.

I was secretly delighted that I'd have an entire day to myself. I would book a massage, facial and pedicure and spend the afternoon by the pool. Now that I was beyond the twelve-week mark it was safe to have a massage.

"You know what Dad, I think I'll spend the day here at the Old Course Hotel and lie by the pool and relax. Do you mind?" I asked.

"No Beans of course not," Dad said as he hugged me. "I think that'll do you some good. You've been working too hard lately according to your mother." Mum had obviously asked my father to get me to relax a little, thinking it was all work-related stress.

"Let's have breakfast together at eight o'clock tomorrow in the conservatory," Dad suggested.

"Great, looking forward to it. Dad it's special to be with you." I kissed him goodnight and Benjamin and I made our way back to our hotel room.

It was only once we had unpacked and showered that I noticed the bottle of Bollinger and two crystal glasses with a note on the table by the window.

"Look," I said to Benjamin.

"Who is that from?" Benjamin asked.

"It is from Dad, the note reads…" I said as I read the note out aloud.

Thought you two might enjoy a little bubbly to ease into your birthday tomorrow, Beans.

Yours Dad

"How ironic if only your father knew there is a more compelling reason for champagne!" Benjamin said.

"I'll leave a message at the B&B where he is staying to say thanks. That way he'll get the message before he goes to bed tonight," I suggested.

We ate breakfast early the following morning in the conservatory at the Old Course Hotel, which lay adjacent to the ninth fairway.

"Happy Birthday Beans," Dad said as we walked into the conservatory. "You got the champagne I see by your note last evening. Here's something small from Mum and I," he added as we settled down to our breakfasts.

I was famished. I scoffed down a bacon and honey waffle with fruit and orange juice while Benjamin had a full English breakfast as did my father.

"Is this conservatory used for target practice?" Benjamin asked my father while I unwrapped my present.

"Why?" Dad asked.

"The glass must need replacing every month by the looks of things," Benjamin said. The shatterproof glass windows of the conservatory had, but for three panes, all been smashed by flying golf balls. We all laughed.

"Beans since when did you eat red meat?"

I had given up eating red meat ten years ago, but since falling pregnant had a craving for meat especially bacon and fillet.

"Oh, just recently. Gives me an excuse to drink red wine," I said as casually as I could. "Dad, the handbag is gorgeous. Bet you chose it personally?" Dad was not one for shopping so I knew he hadn't probably seen it himself. "Here, take a look at what you gave me," I said jokingly.

Just then my stomach began to heave, I knew what was coming.

"Excuse me a moment," I said as I ran to the toilets nearby.

The entire contents of my breakfast came back to pay me a visit. Oh heck!

I now carried breath peppermints with me at all times and put two into my mouth to get rid of the taste. I couldn't quite go back to our room to brush my teeth; Dad would know there was something fishy going on, so I walked back to our table in as easy a manner as I could muster.

"Are you alright Emma?" Dad asked.

"Just peachy. I took my multi-vitamin this morning on an empty stomach, you know what happens if you're stupid enough as I am to do that," I lied.

"Emma, we should be finished golf by two o'clock. Would you like to join us for a late lunch at the club house?" Dad asked.

"Sure, thought I'd walk a little first then swim a few laps in the indoor pool. I'll come from there," I said, glad to have some time to reflect. As it turned out I never made the walk and fell asleep on our bed instead. I did however manage to go for a swim.

That afternoon my father suggested he take us for a drive in the car and show us around the town of St Andrews. We could have gone on foot, the town being small enough, but there were rain clouds in the sky.

As we were driving through the town I decided then was as good a time as ever to tell my father that I was pregnant. To be honest I couldn't keep the news from him for much longer, I had been dying to tell Mum for months.

I hadn't consulted Benjamin as to when I would break the news, but he knew I'd tell Dad sometime that day, being my birthday.

"Prince William studied here," Benjamin said. "Must be a good university then!"

"Dad," I said tentatively, as we drove past the university. Dad was explaining how the university has no campus as such but is integrated into the town itself.

"Yes Beans."

"I've some news to tell you," I said.

"Mmm," Dad said, as he continued to drive chatting to Benjamin in the passenger seat.

"I'm pregnant," I said, without any warning it came at him like a bullet.

Dad swerved and then corrected the car.

"I think I'll pull over," Dad said.

"Wait, that's not all Dad. I've two buns in the oven," I added, my timing not exactly perfect as he almost crashed head on into an oncoming vehicle.

"I'm definitely stopping now!" Dad said, quite ruffled as he pulled the car over to the side of the road.

"Did I hear you correctly Beans?" Dad asked, looking at me from over the car seat.

"Yes you most certainly did," I laughed.

"What is it you young people take nowadays to be so fertile?" he asked jokingly.

I think he was so stunned that he wasn't quite sure how to react. Instead of congratulating us he sat silently for a short whilst glaring at the steering wheel.

"I don't think we've got twins in the family," he added, obviously wondering how in the world I could land up with two babies inside me. I thought I'd save him the agony and decided to explain.

"Dad, I had fertility treatment, not IVF something less dramatic but along those lines. That's why I'm carrying two. You're right there's no history of twins on either side. It wasn't an immaculate conception," trying to help put his mind at rest.

"What's IVF? Sounds gibberish to me. I know your mother wanted grandchildren but couldn't you do it one at a time Emma?" he asked, still shocked by the news. Both Benjamin and I laughed.

"Paul, it stands for in vitro fertilisation. Not that that means anything to you either I'm sure. Basically, Emma needed help ovulating and she found that help through an Assisted Conception Unit in London," Benjamin explained.

"I think I'm too old to want to know more about it right now. Let me digest the news. The bottle of bubbly was co-incidental then wasn't it Beans?" he added.

"Yes it was." I felt a little lost. I hadn't known what to expect from my father but certainly not such bewilderment. Surely he knew at some point his little girl might have babies of her own?

Dad started up the engine again and asked us if we wanted to see the new St Andrews Bay Golf Resort and Spa.

We said yes and I could sense him starting to get his head around our news.

"How many months, Emma?" Dad asked, now a little more at ease.

"Thirteen weeks. We haven't told anyone until now." I thought I'd keep the news of the nuchal scan at bay for fear of my father having a possible heart attack.

When we arrived at the new golfing resort Dad came over to me as I stepped out of the car and motioned as if to hug me, but then hesitated.

"I'm not breakable, you can give me a huge hug. I'd like it if you did," I said.

With that my father gave me the biggest hug he's ever given me and whispered, "Congratulations! I'm going to be a grandfather twice over," in my ear.

I noticed his eyes became watery. He was clearly moved beyond words.

"You know I never do things in half measures," I smiled.

"We thought we'd catch up with our friends whose children are out of nappies already and onto their second and third children now." Benjamin beamed as he shook hands and hugged him.

"Well done you two!" Dad finally said out loud for anyone to hear. "No wonder you've filled out a bit, so it wasn't the English cuisine after all," now putting the pieces together in his head.

"Let's call your mother tonight before dinner," Dad suggested as we headed back to the hotel.

We had dinner at a quaint, local fish restaurant near the water. Dad had booked a quiet table for us next to the window with a seaside view. It was raining and the sky dark and ominous looking. We had stopped by the Royal and Ancient clubhouse on the way to collect a bottle of R&A whisky for Benjamin which Dad had bought especially. Women were strictly forbidden as members, so I wandered aimlessly, umbrella in hand, thinking perhaps I might have been caught up in a time warp, the nineteenth century perhaps!

Dad went into the clubhouse and Benjamin waited in the foyer of the clubhouse. I sometimes wondered what went on in those all male clubs seeing that women weren't allowed entry.

"Dad?" I asked, as he came back out carrying a bottle of the finest R&A whisky just for Benjamin.

"Yes, Beans," he replied as we walked over to the restaurant nearby.

"What goes on behind these exclusive men's club doors since women strictly aren't allowed?" I asked facetiously.

"Oh just a bunch of old men trying to escape their wives for a few hours!"

We sat down at our table and I began to dial Mum. I was so excited to tell her the news I had kept secret for three months then.

"Hi Mum."

"Emma, I'm so glad you called. I tried reaching you at the hotel to wish you a happy birthday but just missed you. Have you had a special day with Dad?"

"Yes very. I've got some very exciting news for you," I said eagerly. "I'm pregnant Mum." I'm not sure what kind of reaction I had expected from her either, these being her first grandchildren, especially after the unexpected response from my father.

After a long pause and a few sniffles Mum responded.

"I can't believe it. That's wonderful news. I thought you would never have babies, it's taken so long."

"I know. It's not always easy, these things take time," I said with a touch of irony in my voice. I wanted so badly to share the bad news with someone, the news about the nuchal scan. I needed Mum to comfort and reassure me. I decided to share this news with her too.

"I have other news too. I'm carrying twins," I added, now for sure she'd collapse!

I heard nothing, stunned silence on the other end of the phone.

"Mum, are you alive? Say something, anything."

"I'm a little taken aback, how did that happen?" she asked disbelievingly.

Benjamin could see my face drop and knew that Mum had hurt my feelings in some way. This was not unusual, it's the sort of relationship I had with my mother. We often seemed to hurt each other unintentionally.

I felt Benjamin's foot touch mine under the table and he winked.

"A long story Mum, the short of it is I had assistance in falling pregnant which carried a risk of multiples. It was unusual though to have two eggs fertilise," I added, like a child trying to justify their actions to a domineering parent. I'm not sure what compelled me at the time, but even though I should have known then by Mum's initial reaction not to go on and break the bad news. I did, a decision I later regretted.

"You can't possibly have an abnormal child!" Mum exploded. "Do you know what it's like to raise a child with Down's?" The question tore into my heart.

"Slow down. It is not definite. The scan only shows a slightly increased risk, it doesn't mean it's going to be the case." I tried to get her to relax and to look at the positive side, but found myself becoming too emotional.

"Could it be because you had fertility treatment when it wasn't supposed to be?" She pressed on, focusing on all the possible negatives, clouding any joy I had of the fact that I had miraculously managed to conceive despite the odds against us.

"I don't think it's anything to worry about Judy." Benjamin had taken the phone from me; concerned I was becoming too upset. I turned to my father who stood up from the table and walked over to my seat, he lent down and gave me a huge hug.

"Your mother doesn't mean to hurt your feelings. It's her way of showing how much she loves you."

I knew this, but I also knew that I needed someone to confide in, not someone to lecture me on the good versus the bad in everything.

The next telephone call was to Aunt Viv.

"Viv, it's Emma, I've got some exciting news to tell you," relieved to hear her voice.

"Judy, is that you?" Viv asked thinking it was Mum.

"No, it's Emma-Beez, your favourite niece, don't tell me you've forgotten me already?"

"No, no of course not. Where are you, how's your hockey going darling?" Viv was living in the golden years of her life. I didn't want to spoil that image in her mind.

"Fine, thanks. I just wanted to tell you that I love you very very much and that I can't wait to see you. You better be good or I won't bring you your Turkish Delights." Viv adored Turkish Delight. I couldn't bring myself to take her mind away from where it was and impart a sense of reality. So I didn't tell her my exciting news. Just listening to her voice was enough comfort.

"How wonderful, they're my favourite," Viv said.

"Yes, I know."

By the time we left St Andrews for Fort William I felt closer to Dad than I ever had. He had assumed a gentler manner and I could sense a difference in his regard for me. Perhaps it was that his 'little girl' had finally advanced into true womanhood. Mum was also overjoyed and I knew this although her way of showing it was ambiguous.

Benjamin and I spent seven days based at Inverlochy Castle, where we rekindled our love for one another, spending long hours outdoors walking and talking, sleeping or making love until noon, dining out and exploring the Scottish Highlands. It felt good to be alive, we forgot about the decision that had burdened us, and we lived for the moment.

Late one afternoon, our last day in Scotland, having just returned from a day trip to the Isle of Skye, we lay on our bed talking of the day's events, randomly switching channels on the television, when Benjamin suddenly stopped at a channel about identical twins. Thinking this would be of interest to me he decided to pause for a moment.

"This looks interesting. Shall we watch a while?"

"Sure," I said somewhat indifferent.

As the programme progressed it became obvious that this was not only a programme about twins but about the increasing occurrence of Down's Syndrome amongst twins particularly identical twins.

Suddenly we were reminded of the dilemma we faced.

"Could this be a message of sorts?" I asked Benjamin.

"It may be. Perhaps we should talk about the subject before we leave tomorrow and go back to London?" Benjamin quietly suggested. "I'll turn this off though, it's depressing."

"I've already made up my mind, sweetheart. I thought I'd tell you on the plane but now is as good a time as any," I said, shaking a little. I had given it some thought that day and had probably known long before Scotland what my heart was telling me to do anyway.

"I'm going to have the amniocentesis. Even if I wait until twenty weeks and the scan then comes back normal, I am still at a far higher risk with twin two than I am with twin one. I'll lie awake at night wondering if I don't and never forgive myself if we do have an abnormal child."

"Are you sure Emma?"

"Yes, positive. I don't think I could raise a child who was handicapped and although I know it's not what I should be feeling because of the gift that God has given us, I can't pretend I don't feel this way," I said, feeling awkward that I could appear so unappreciative and selfish.

"I must admit I'm relieved Emma. I support your decision and whatever happens remember we have each other." He kissed me on the forehead.

Chapter Eight

Coopers and Co. had been hard hit in recent months by the downturn in the market; business was getting tougher and deals fewer. As a result all offices around the world had undergone a series of retrenchments. Returning from our ten-day break to a depressed and unmotivated working environment was not easy. I had decided together with Benjamin that I would tell Mark I was pregnant on our return from Scotland. I was expanding daily; I couldn't hide the bump for much longer and, fearing people would think I was letting myself go and getting fat, I knew I had to tell Mark soon.

If I had wanted to crucify my career then and there it would have been to tell Mark during that retrenchment week, so I left if for the following week.

Finally, a week later I approached Mark.

"Mark I've got to talk to you. I've some exciting news to share with you."

"Emma, I've been meaning to set up a time for you and I to catch up on things while you've been away and before I go on leave myself for two weeks," Mark said. "So what's up?"

"I'm expecting twins. I'm fifteen weeks pregnant." He glanced down at my stomach and smiled. He didn't appear in the least bit surprised.

"I thought so Emma, you were putting on weight and for someone who never puts on weight I had already guessed." Mark had three small children of his own, a family man at heart. "Congratulations," he came over and kissed me twice, once on each cheek. My pregnancy obviously wasn't as inconspicuous as I had thought.

"We're ecstatic, although Benjamin is a little nervous," I said truthfully.

"Tell Benjamin he's done well. Are there twins in the family?" The inevitable question, always asked whenever anyone has twins and the one I resented most. How should one respond? Should I tell the truth or should I lie and say yes but distant on Benjamin's side? The latter would help dispense of further questions and prying minds eager to understand why I had to have fertility. I still regarded fertility treatment as the sign of failure.

"No. I plan to take maternity leave in March if that's possible," I said, and left it there for Mark to wonder how, why and what.

"Mmm, yes of course. I'll talk to Human Resources and ensure all proper procedures are followed." He looked at his watch. Picking that up as a sign I suggested, "Let's catch up on current issues and upcoming ones so I can pick up straight away."

"Sure." Mark and I spent a good hour and a half catching up and planning. We also had budgets to produce while he was on leave, which fell to me to complete. "Oh lastly, I've told Jonathan that I'm resigning effective January next year right before you go on maternity leave." Jonathan was our managing director.

"How did he take the news?" I asked, curious as to his response.

"Not badly surprisingly. I may consult for a few weeks after that until a replacement is found." Mark did not add but he knew I understood, that it would be impossible now for me to take up his role if I was going on maternity leave. What he didn't say was that the company would see my pregnancy as the beginning of the end of my career and the start of full time motherhood. That's the way they saw things unfortunately, black or white, and there was little room for lateral and creative thought when it came to working mothers with young families. There simply weren't any at a senior level.

"I'll make sure I coach someone to temporarily take on my responsibilities while I'm on maternity leave and who will step down once I return." I already had that person in mind.

The person I had in mind for the role, an outside consultant whom I had contracted in for a few months to work with me on a number of initiatives and to ease the work load, there being no budget for new hires, was the perfect fit or so I thought at the time.

One weakness of mine, one Benjamin always cautioned me about, was my trusting nature of people, the very same people who often had hidden agendas. I brushed him off thinking he was too pessimistic because he was paid to be sceptical at work. I was to learn a valuable lesson in the months to come and one I'd never repeat.

Benjamin and I had arranged to meet at the doctor's rooms for the amniocentesis. I arrived half and hour early, coming straight from home. I was nervous so decided to window shop, walking up and down the pavements around Harley Street and Marylebone. Not terribly exciting but it beat sitting in a waiting room biting my nails for half an hour.

I saw the cab arrive and Benjamin stepped out. As he paid the driver I called to him to let him know I was walking back down the street. He did look dashing in his suit, pink checked shirt and purple tie.

He wasn't wearing his jacket, so I noticed his armpits were a little wet. He was nervous too or he had had a difficult morning at work.

"How are you doing?" He hugged me, and we walked into the doctor's rooms together.

"So... so. Do you think I could be put under for this procedure?"

"No, but we could arrange a little gin for you to numb the senses a bit." I had done my reading and knew what to expect. As it turned out my eyes were tightly shut throughout the procedure, so I didn't get to see any of it anyway!

"Mr Hogan, are you sure you want to stay in the room for this?" Dr Geoffrey asked as I made myself comfortable on the examination table – familiar with this part of the proceedings anyway.

"Yes absolutely, I'll be fine," Benjamin said, really sure of himself.

"Fine. Please stand over to that corner of the bed. You can hold Mrs Hogan's hand if you wish. Now, Mrs Hogan I'm going to explain what I'm going to do today." Dr Geoffrey positioned himself on a stool beside the examination table.

"You need to sit really still for the entire procedure which will take about half an hour. I will first anaesthetise your tummy with a local injection. I then use ultrasound to see where the babies are lying so that I safely pierce the walls of the abdomen and womb and enter the amniotic fluid in which your babies are floating without harming them in any way. I then take a little fluid from each sac with a syringe and this is then sent off to the lab for testing." Oh heck I thought to myself, he has to trust technology! I knew all too well, how fast things go south if the technology fails.

"How many times have you performed an amnio without an ensuing miscarriage?" I could not help asking him the question, which might have appeared an insult to his competence, but I needed the reassurance.

"This is my first," he said with a twinkle in his eye. There was a deathly silence.

"You needn't worry, Mrs Hogan, I can assure you I've only ever had one patient experience a miscarriage and I've performed thousands."

"May I close my eyes please, I hate needles of any form?" I asked, ready to faint just hearing the details of the procedure.

"Of course, whatever makes you feel more at ease." Dr Geoffrey began to get organised. At this point I looked back over my shoulder at Benjamin.

"You go ahead, darling, I'll let you know how the babies handle everything." Benjamin sounded too confident for my liking.

I saw the image of my babies on the screen as Dr Geoffrey moved the probe over my tummy to locate the babies' positions and to see their movements. Both foetuses were active, legs and arms moving peacefully in the fluid they knew as their home. Snug and contented. Little did they know what was coming, their environment would be disturbed and all I could do was pray they'd keep still.

"Right, are you ready, Mrs Hogan?" Dr Geoffrey asked.

"As ready as I'll ever be." That was the signal to close my eyes. I felt Benjamin's grip on my hand tighten.

"Good luck, darling, I'm right here," he whispered in my ear.

I felt the local anaesthetic and I felt something pierce my tummy. Phew I thought, it's not so bad. But as Dr Geoffrey continued to move the needle around, so I began to feel less and less comfortable. It was not unbearable, but close.

"There all over," Dr Geoffrey said, just as I thought I could take no more. Before I could open my eyes I suddenly heard a thud as if something had hit the ground. It had, and it was my husband, Benjamin had fainted!

"Are you alright, Mr Hogan?" Dr Geoffrey had rushed to see if he was conscious.

"Mmm," he paused. "I think I'm fine. I lost my balance." Benjamin, the supportive husband, had watched the entire procedure, which had obviously been too much for him to handle. Immediately, the needle the size of a knitting needle, had been removed from my tummy, Benjamin's wits had failed him and he had fallen to the ground.

"I didn't know I'd have to be more concerned about you, Mr Hogan, than I would about your wife!" Dr Geoffrey said light-heartedly.

Benjamin relayed the entire procedure to me during the cab ride back to our apartment. I had asked Mark if I could take two days sick leave to recover from the amnio as I was advised to do so.

"It was as if they knew," Benjamin said. "The minute the needle pierced the first sac both babies stopped moving and they lay there still as can be for the entire time."

It did take me a good two days to fully recover. I felt weak and my tummy felt really tender.

Although I had taken two days' sick leave, I was working while in bed, taking calls and speaking to clients.

I resigned myself to the fact that if I got through the next two days without bleeding and any other warning signs of a miscarriage, then I just had to get through the next ten days waiting for the results to come back.

I was beginning to understand why my friends had said pregnancy was a waiting game; it's all about patience. I seemed to wait for something every step of the way. The anxiety almost prevented me from truly enjoying my pregnancy. Perhaps this was because it was my first and I simply had no idea what lay ahead.

And furthermore it's a fallacy that women are at their best during pregnancy. The only glow I had, was the skin on my tummy, which glowed as it continued to stretch beyond my wildest imagination.

I put the proposal to Jenny Green, the consultant I wanted to step in for me while I was on maternity leave.

"Sure, sounds good to me. Your position is secure. I won't let you down," Jenny had responded.

I had mentioned to Jenny that she would not earn what she had in the past. Times were tough and her daily rate was way too high. Jenny accepted the revised figures and I felt pleased with myself that I had managed to arrange a competent replacement for the time I would be away. Someone I felt I trusted and who would not screw up.

Benjamin and I had been house hunting for months. The three-bedroom apartment in Kensington Green was no longer suitable for our rapidly expanding family. We decided to look further out of London. Somewhere we could afford with a garage, a small garden and a short travelling distance from London for Benjamin's work and mine.

Now, contrary to most people we had come across in the UK and most of our friends in fact, we were not looking for a period home. They were generally high maintenance, like a mistress in need of constant attention and pampering. Instead we were looking for a new build, something in keeping with period homes but brand new. I also didn't warm to the idea of spending days or even months cleaning someone else's dirt and grime of many years, especially in my condition.

"You must be due anytime now," the estate agent, Tom, said as we walked out of the one home we came to view.

"No, actually I'm only eighteen weeks pregnant. I am carrying two though," I added, so he didn't feel too bad. He blushed none-the-less.

"I'm sorry, difficult to tell nowadays. Some women have no stomach at all and give birth the next day." Tom tried to climb out of the hole he had dug himself into.

Benjamin and I decided to stay a little longer in Wimbledon and take a walk in the park before driving back to London.

"I can't believe the prices you pay for property here," I said to Benjamin, comparing them to those in South Africa, admittedly not a fair comparison.

"I know. We could buy a shopping mall for the same price as some of these four bedroom homes. But we're not comparing apples with apples," Benjamin said. "I think we'll have to look even further out. Clearly Wimbledon prices reflect the fact that it's the home of tennis."

"I don't want to live in the sticks, Benjamin, and feel lonely everyday!" I protested, not wanting to move any further out of London having only recently moved to the UK.

It took us another month before we finally settled on a property in Horsell, a little village in Woking. Ideal for Benjamin and I in that the commute into the City only took twenty-five minutes, yet we could enjoy some of the luxuries of home such as a garden and a driveway with a garage.

I didn't understand how all the mothers in London did it without parking near their apartments, what with children, prams and shopping bags. It was hell especially in wet weather.

You'd have to be Posh and Becks to afford a home with a driveway in Kensington or Chelsea!

"Mum we've found a property. If the purchase goes through, which could take as long as a prison sentence in this country, will you help us move?" I would be around twenty-eight weeks and unable to do my shoelaces up let alone move furniture. As it was Benjamin had to cut my toenails each fortnight.

"Of course. Dad and I'll be coming over for Christmas this year," she said.

I loved my mother; she always came up trumps.

I heard the results of the amnio at work late one afternoon.

"Mrs Hogan I'm sorry to disturb you it's Dr Geoffrey, I have your amnio results."

My hand shook for a moment and I asked him to hang on as I walked into an empty meeting room and closed the door behind me. A good half of me did not want to know the results.

"Yes, Dr Geoffrey, go ahead," I said, now safely out of earshot.

"It's good news. The results only came back fifteen minutes ago, I wanted to tell you straight away." As he said this, my heart rose and I began to cry. I cried for all the nights Benjamin and I had lain awake wondering if I was carrying an abnormal child. I cried for all the parents who weren't as fortunate as we were. I cried for the sheer joy of knowing everything was going to work out fine.

"Do you want to know the sexes?" Dr Geoffrey asked.

We hadn't discussed this. I didn't even know what Benjamin would have said.

"Yes I would." Suddenly I felt so close to my unborn babies, they had become little people already. I needed to know what gender they were.

"You are going to have a little girl and a little boy, one of each," Dr Geoffrey said with an unusual element of excitement in his voice.

"Oh, thank you, thank you so very very much," I said. I'm going to have a pigeon pair, could I ask for much more?

By the time I reached thirty-three weeks, my breasts had grown to the size of udders and my veins were bluer than the blood of Royals. They resembled major highways on a road map. I had had to start working from home and only went into the City for the occasional meeting. I waddled everywhere I went and had to sit with my legs wide apart to make way for my enormous stomach. I felt decidedly elegant of course! Colleagues had jokingly asked whom I had bribed to have such a large stomach.

At each bi-monthly scan I had asked Dr Geoffrey if he thought I'd make it to thirty-seven weeks. I wanted to carry as long as I could, I knew that if they came early, there would be complications.

Meanwhile I had been coaching Jenny Green to take over my responsibilities while I was on maternity leave. I had also given her the heads up about the initiatives I had wanted to get approved by the board during the period I was away and when I returned. These initiatives Jenny had promised to work on and progress in my absence. I felt relieved that I had found someone who would protect my position and at the same time had the competence to progress these new initiatives.

The company had undergone yet another internal restructure at the executive level, which did not make things easy for Jenny. Not only was her reporting line a moving target so were her set of responsibilities as it turned out. Mark had officially left the company in February just before my maternity leave began. Allan Crawford took over his responsibilities and became Global Head of Sales and Marketing. Allan would be Jenny's boss, well her boss for the time being anyway until another restructure occurred.

Politics and more politics, I chuckled to myself, being at liberty now to see the amusing side of it all. I had had three different bosses in the past two years, all of whom had carried different titles. If I blinked long enough, I'd miss the next restructure.

I arranged with Mark and Jenny to have our last working lunch at home to discuss my final hand-over. I was thirty-four weeks pregnant and so heavy that I could barely climb the stairs without feeling like I'd topple backwards at any given moment. If anyone had made a caricature of me I'm sure they would have used Humpty Dumpty as their inspiration.

That day for some reason I felt particularly weak and uncomfortable. I couldn't sit for long periods so excused my behaviour and asked Mark and Jenny if they wouldn't mind if I walked around now and again, sitting had become excruciating. It felt as if twin one's head was already sitting between my knees.

"I'm not sure I'll cope with labour pains if this is just the Braxton Hicks contractions," I said jokingly.

"Emma, we're almost through. Let's fast track the last few items to discuss so you can get some rest. It's been a long day for you now." Mark's suggestion came as a huge relief.

"That would be great if you've got what you need Jenny to run with things?" I asked pacing the floor.

"Emma, that's all. I think I'll cope. You're also just at the other end of a telephone line too if I need you." Jenny sounded confident.

I was relieved to see their car drive out of our driveway; I was really feeling very uncomfortable. What I hadn't and dared not mention was that I had been leaking all afternoon. Perhaps I was becoming incontinent? Hundreds of thoughts ran through my mind and I began to panic.

No, I'm not going to have these babies now, it's too soon I kept telling myself. I knew there would be problems if they came early. Mum had told me I should be in bed resting from thirty-two weeks, but as usual I hadn't take any notice. So I climbed up the stairs, leaving all the lunch dishes to be sorted later, and without taking any of my clothes off crawled onto our bed and nestled under the covers.

It didn't take long before I was fast asleep. My sleep was broken though. I kept turning from one side to the other moving the pregnancy pillow to and fro as I desperately tried to overcome that excruciating pain, which seemed to penetrate my entire being.

Oh Lord, please don't let these babies come now. Keep them safe inside for another three weeks.

Benjamin arrived home; I could vaguely hear the front door open and his footsteps as he ascended the staircase towards our bedroom. The house was dark being wintertime and I hadn't turned any lights on.

"Emma?" I heard Benjamin call out.

"I'm in here, in bed," I said, reassured that my husband was now home.

"What's the matter?" Benjamin asked as he sat on the bed beside me and felt my head to check for a fever.

"I'm in pain and I've been leaking fluid all day. I'm not sure what's going on," I said, tears in my eyes. Deep down I think I knew what was happening but continued to deny it.

"Shall I call Dr Geoffrey?" Benjamin asked as he picked up the receiver.

"No! Please don't darling; I'm fine it's the Braxton Hicks contractions I think. Don't you remember in the antenatal classes they spoke of false alarms? Well I think this is one of them."

"Are you sure Emma?" Benjamin sounded sceptical.

"Yes. Tell me about your day?" I changed the subject.

"It was fine. Shall I make you supper and bring you dinner in bed tonight?" Benjamin asked, never eager to rehash his day at work.

"That would be great. I'm sorry I left the kitchen in a state of chaos after my lunch meeting, I've been in bed since then," I apologised.

"What's this?" Benjamin asked as he put his hand on the mattress to push himself up.

"Oh, that's where I've been leaking. I'll change the sheets," I said embarrassed.

"I'm going to listen to you Emma, but if this pain gets any worse, we're going to the hospital do you hear me?" Benjamin sounded scared. "And you are not doing anything of the sort. The sheets can stay like this until you're feeling better."

It hadn't occurred to me then that if I had only listened to my body and gone into the hospital, Dr Geoffrey might have managed to keep the babies in for a week or so longer by prescribing drugs.

PART TWO

Chapter Nine

I felt progressively worse as the day rolled on.

That night after dinner before going to bed, I went to the bathroom to get ready.

"Benjamin!" I screamed.

"Emma, what's wrong?" Benjamin came running into the bathroom.

I showed him my underwear soaked in blood.

"Oh my God Emma, are we too late how long have you been bleeding for?" he asked totally beside himself.

"This is the first sign of blood. I think we need to call the hospital right away. They're coming, I can't keep them in any longer. I'm sorry." I was devastated. I had failed.

From then on in, everything was a blur. We packed my overnight bag in twenty seconds flat. Something I should have done weeks before but kept putting off in the vague hope that it would delay the babies' arrival. The gorgeous nightshirts I had bought especially for my stay in hospital, never made it into the overnight bag, there wasn't enough time.

Benjamin became Superman overnight. He carried me down the stairs and lifted me into the car. Me and the extra eighteen kilos I had put on since conceiving.

Fortunately it was late at night so the traffic into London wasn't too bad. Each time Benjamin drove over a bump through Kensington making his way towards St Mary's Hospital, I screamed out in agony.

The pain so piercing seemed unbearable and just when I thought I would die the contractions would cease just long enough for me to gain my breath and then they would start all over again.

It felt like the first twin was half out already and her head sandwiched between my legs.

As soon as I arrived at the hospital the staff in the Lindo Wing, who had been contacted ahead of time by the main switchboard, were there to greet us as we entered the building.

I was bundled into a wheelchair and taken in the elevator upstairs.

"Mrs Hogan we're going to take you and your husband to a vacant room for now while we try to locate an empty room on the third floor for you after delivery," the nursing sister said. "We have notified Dr Geoffrey and I need to measure how far dilated you are before we call him again," she continued.

"Emma, are you alright?" Benjamin asked.

"No, I'm in real pain. Can someone please get me something for the pain? I need it now!" I demanded.

"I'm sorry Mrs Hogan we cannot give you any medication until the doctor arrives. Now we are going to help you up onto the bed to see how far dilated you are," she said as she, Benjamin and another night nurse picked me up and laid me onto the bed.

All I could think of while the sister busied herself measuring how far along I was, was about the consequence of having done nothing sooner. It was my entire fault. Stubborn, selfish me! What would happen if the babies had had a lack of oxygen since the night before? What would happen if they had contracted an infection?

"Right, call Dr Geoffrey, she's quite far along already. She's seven centimetres dilated. When did these contractions start Mrs Hogan?" the nurse asked.

Forever, was all I could think.

"Monday." Ben answered on my behalf.

"Why didn't you contact the hospital then?" she asked.

Why was she asking me these stupid questions? It was pointless. I didn't contact them earlier but I was there, that should be good enough. It was terrible knowing that I could have prevented their early arrival by doing something sooner; I didn't need my nose rubbed in it too.

"I thought they were just Braxton Hicks contractions. I didn't want the babies early." I burst into tears, the ceiling seemed to cave in on me; everything was happening far too quickly. I wasn't ready. Just give me three more weeks, please!

"Mrs Hogan, so you couldn't wait could you?" Dr Geoffrey had arrived. How he arrived so soon I would never know, perhaps he had been helicoptered into the building.

"I know. I tried but they just couldn't wait any longer I suppose. Please, I need something for the pain I can't take much more," I pleaded.

Dr Geoffrey examined me before responding. He pulled Benjamin aside and said something to him then turned to me.

"Mrs Hogan your waters broke around twenty-four hours ago, you're seven centimetres dilated and I am concerned about infection. I'm afraid I'm going to have to perform an emergency C-Section. I need to get them out, especially twin number one," Dr Geoffrey said earnestly.

I looked up at Benjamin who simply squeezed my hand and whispered, "It's going to be fine, Emma. Our babies want out, the hospital will take care of them."

"Yes go ahead." As I said this I felt like I was falling out of a plane and could not stop myself. Everything was happening around me as if I was watching from afar, my mind elevated above my own body. It's too soon. It's too soon! The ground was coming up towards me, consuming me as I saw my body hurtling downwards.

Dr Geoffrey, Benjamin and a nurse then wheeled me down a dark and cold underground passageway to the other side of the hospital. I was wrapped in two blankets yet felt completely naked.

I held my stomach and in my mind massaged my babies as I stroked my tummy, telling them quietly that they were going to be just fine, that Mummy would take care of them.

Strange how even in such a delirious state my maternal instincts took over. I could barely string a sentence together but in my mind I was carrying on a conversation with my unborn children.

I was given gas while waiting for the anaesthetist to arrive to administer the epidural. It made me feel sick, dizzy, and nauseous even suicidal.

"Please, no more gas."

He asked the nurse to take the gas away by which time I felt numb, a prisoner to the medical staff around me. They could have done anything at this point, I would not have been able to protest, I felt so incredibly weak.

"Emma, you need to sit upright." I heard Benjamin's voice amongst the humdrum of a dozen or so others. Apparently, I heard later, there was a football team of people in the theatre all busy around us.

A nurse stood in front of me and Benjamin stood by my side, while I could hear a man's voice behind me. The nurse kept pulling me towards her and asking me to lean forward.

"I can't. That's as far as I can go!" I screamed in agony.

How could they expect me to lean forward, I was carrying five rugby balls in front of me which didn't deflate!

In between all of this I felt the contractions getting closer and more painful. I felt like a piece of ham in a sandwich squeezed inside a lunchbox between two large cans of coca-cola.

"Almost there Mrs Hogan just sit still for me will you!" the male voice said firmly, when finally I felt the needle penetrate the space between the vertebrae in my back.

I felt a cool liquid permeate my body. Slowly the pain started to subside and I felt nothing, absolutely nothing. It was the strangest sensation. I imagined this must be what it felt like to be on a high.

Where had Benjamin gone? Only then did I realise that I wasn't holding Benjamin's hand any longer. Instead I was squeezing Dr Geoffrey's who gently put my hand by my side as I turned to see Benjamin walk back into the theatre.

I tried to speak but no words came out of my mouth. I tried again.

"Where were you?" I asked, when I could finally string a sentence together.

"I had to get some air, no need to worry," Benjamin reassured me.

I felt very little from then on in except I did feel Dr Geoffrey's hands rummaging around in my stomach.

"Congratulations, Mrs Hogan, here's your little girl," Dr Geoffrey said as he passed my little baby girl to me.

Hey, this is easy I thought, no pushing, no screaming, and no more excruciating pain!

I held this little fragile, wet and screaming body in my arms for a moment and kissed her forehead. I knew instinctively then that she was small but without my contact lenses in I couldn't really tell how small. I was moved beyond imagination. I turned my head towards Benjamin who had tears in his eyes.

There was a pause and I heard nothing.

"What about my little boy?" I asked worried that something had happened to him on the way out.

"Here he is darling." Benjamin passed him to me. I held him for only a brief moment then he was taken away. I barely caught a glimpse of his little fragile body. He was small but nothing could have prepared me for how small my little baby boy really was.

"What's wrong, why are they taking them away?" I panicked.

"Everything's going to be fine, Emma; they just need to do a few tests on them first. You'll see them shortly." Benjamin spoke quietly and then I heard him whisper something to Dr Geoffrey.

After thirty-four weeks of pregnancy, it took all of two minutes to deliver Jessica and William. I was suddenly overcome by a sense of emptiness, of incompleteness. Two bodies I had carried for thirty-four weeks, which had become part of me, were no longer inside me.

Jessica was then brought to me and laid gently on my chest while I waited to be wheeled back to the Lindo Wing, to my room. William had to undergo further tests.

"Is he going to be alright?" I asked Benjamin.

"He'll be fine, you just hold Jessica. I'll stay with William," Benjamin said.

Jessica and I lay there together in the cold dark passageway outside the theatre waiting for what I did not know. In the silence of that moment I took hold of her tiny weenie hand and encased it in mine. I kissed her forehead as she cried and wrapped her up so she could hear the beating of my heart. I had read that within minutes after birth a baby's natural instinct is to seek their mother's breast and to suckle. I waited for Jessica to seek mine, but she didn't move, she just lay there crying.

"Put her to your breast," the nursing sister said, as she appeared from nowhere and began wheeling me to my room.

"I'm trying, but she doesn't seem to know what to do. She seems tired and bewildered." I could sense that Jessica, although she had clearly wanted out, was totally overwhelmed by this strange place wherein she now found herself. I didn't want to cause her further stress by forcing her, so I just held her close.

I later learned that a baby only fully develops their sucking, swallowing and breathing co-ordination at around thirty-six weeks, so it was understandable that what should have been instinctive behaviour for Jessica, didn't come until weeks later, once she had grown a little and passed the thirty-six week mark.

What I know now, however, didn't help me in the slightest back then. I kept trying to get Jessica to suckle worried she'd be starving, which clearly she was. This just made me feel like a failure yet again and the harder I tried, the more Jessica resisted and the more upset we both became.

I cried both out of joy of having brought two babies into this world and out of sadness having failed to carry them longer, to give them the nurturing they needed safe inside my womb.

I had read all the books on breast-feeding something that I felt pressured into doing. No consideration or very little for that matter was given to mothers who couldn't breast-feed due perhaps to inverted nipples or illness and no consideration was given to babies who just couldn't get the hang of it. It was only later that I learned one reason is financial. All girls, mothers should I say, under the age of sixteen receive free formula from the State.

I held Jessica on my chest careful not to break her little bones. Her hands were so tiny I could barely see any fingernails. Oh what have I done, she's been born too soon!

The nurses took Jessica away to the nursery so I could get some rest. They told me that they would feed her by nasal gastric tube, something that horrified me to start with. The thought of putting a tube through her nostril down her throat and into her stomach made me cringe. What happened if the tube went down her windpipe? Would she have negative associations with eating for years to come? Would she be able to learn outside of the womb, how to suckle? How long would it take her to catch up?

As I lay in bed waiting for Benjamin to come from the Neonatal Intensive Care Unit where they had taken William, I began to think of the worst possible consequences of having brought two babies into this world six weeks too early.

I was filled with remorse and I was afraid.

"How are you doing?" Benjamin walked into the room just as Dr Geoffrey joined in behind him.

"Mrs Hogan, congratulations. How are you feeling?" Dr Geoffrey asked before I could respond to Benjamin.

I looked over at Benjamin who looked strained and weary. It was three thirty in the morning and neither he nor I had slept for the past twenty-four hours.

I suddenly became aware that I couldn't move. I tried to lift my legs but they were dead. The messages from my brain were not getting through.

"I can't move!" I said, panicking that something had gone horribly wrong with the epidural and I was paralysed.

"That's normal Mrs Hogan. You will regain feeling in your legs in the next four hours and gradually from there you can build up your strength by standing a few minutes and then walking a little. It may take a good seven days before you are up to going home," Dr Geoffrey said.

I felt relieved. I didn't think I could cope with life outside the hospital. I needed a sanctuary for a while, a safe haven in which I could come to terms with what had just transpired in the last twelve hours.

"When can I take a shower?" I felt dirty and perhaps even thought that the water might wash away some of the guilt and sorrow I felt.

"Not today, tomorrow perhaps. The nurses will wash you down each morning and evening. No need to worry," Dr Geoffrey said.

"They are taking good care of your son, William, I believe you have called him, in the Intensive Care Unit." Dr Geoffrey had obviously been to check on William already.

"You will be getting a strong painkiller every twelve hours and in between you can have an epidural top-up, hence why we've left the tube in." I felt something down my back that must have been the tube he was referring to.

"You might also find it easier to sleep for the next three nights by taking a sleeping pill each evening before going to bed. I'll make sure the nurses give you one tonight. I've asked the nurses to take some blood to check your iron levels. You're looking a little pale, Mrs Hogan, which is to be expected. I'll be back to check on you later tonight." Dr Geoffrey shook Benjamin's hand and left the room.

There was silence. It was just Benjamin and me in the room, staring at each other, both traumatised by what we'd been through.

"It's going to be alright Emma. You're a proud mother of two beautiful babies," Benjamin said as he sat down beside me on my bed.

"How's William? Where is he?" I hadn't seen my son as yet, only that brief encounter in the theatre. In a way though I was relieved that I couldn't go anywhere until the next day, I don't think I could have coped with seeing William right then. It was enough knowing that he was smaller than my wildest imagination and weaker than Jessica.

"He's doing well Emma. They have moved him now to the High Care Unit, which is good news. He's on oxygen, something called CPAP, and he is being fed by intravenous tube. He's tiny Emma, but he's adorable." My husband, who never cries, wiped a tear and then another from his face. I was moved; Benjamin needed me just as much as I needed him we would get through this together. We had each other.

"I love you, darling," I said as I lent over and hugged him. We sat there together for ten minutes or more just holding each other, finding comfort in each other's embrace.

"Why is Jessica with me and not in the High Care Unit Benjamin?" I asked, wondering why Jessica, who was also six weeks early, should be brought to me and not kept under constant supervision too, like William.

"I'm not sure. I suppose they like to keep babies near their mothers. She's a lot stronger than William and she weighs more than he does." Benjamin was grappling for straws and he knew he didn't sound convincing.

"We can ask the nurse," Benjamin added. "I've been in to see Jessica and she's asleep now having been fed. I thought I would drive home quickly and fetch some things for you, and I'll be back in time for us to call the rest of the family at a decent hour in South Africa and tell them the good news. You can get an hour or so rest while I'm gone," Benjamin said as he unpacked my overnight bag.

I didn't want to be left alone with my thoughts again. I was frightened.

"Please don't leave me alone. I need your company right now, I'm frightened," I pleaded with Benjamin.

"Emma, I know you're exhausted and you need some sleep. You will feel stronger and better able to deal with everything if you rest a little. I won't be long, promise. What do you need from home?" Benjamin said. I rattled off a list of things I could think of, off the top of my head.

"I think I need a top-up. I can feel the pain building again," I said as the pain pierced every corner of my body.

"I'll buzz the nurse," Benjamin said as he pressed the intercom.

The nurse came and administered the top-up I needed. I felt the cold liquid penetrate the nerve endings in my back as it made its way into my bloodstream. I felt instant relief.

I had fallen asleep almost immediately Benjamin left the room and was finally woken by the sound of cutlery. The nurse had brought my breakfast. I must have slept for a couple of hours; it must be around eight o'clock?

But when I looked at my watch it wasn't quite seven.

Not having been hospitalised for years I had forgotten that the meal times in hospitals coincided with those for a three-year-old!

I was famished. They could have put almost anything in front of me and I would have eaten it.

"I've brought a dual electric breast pump for you, so you can begin expressing straight away. You'll need as much milk as you can produce for those two little babies of yours," the nurse added, and passed me a foreign looking contraption.

What in the world was I to do with this strange object? I had never expressed before and had no idea how it was done.

"You'll have to show me. I'm afraid I've never used one of these things before," I said.

She proceeded to demonstrate how I was to place the suction end over my nipples and areola and once positioned correctly, then ensure the other end was tightly screwed onto the end of the bottle into which I was going to express breast milk. She then showed me how I could increase the suction strength. All terribly technical.

She finished explaining what I had to do, but continued to linger as if she wanted to watch and make sure that I could manage on my own.

"I'll manage on my own thanks," I said, too self-conscious to attempt it in front of her.

I hadn't given the act of breast-feeding much thought. I only knew what the books had said; it was said to be the best form of nutrition for babies for their immunity, to prevent eczema and allergies, to help with development and for bonding. I had nothing to lose, so I thought I'd give it a go, wanting to do the right thing for William and Jessica.

I tried for ten minutes to get milk out of my breast but nothing came. I felt a bit like a cow must feel when a complete novice milks her udders. Bloody uncomfortable!

I decided that perhaps I hadn't increased the suction strength enough so I turned it up to full.

Ouch!

It felt like my nipples were being pinched in a vice grip. How the heck did any woman try long enough to get the hang of this and who in their right minds would persevere?

"How are you getting on?" The nurse entered the room pushing my little Jessica in front of her, at the same time very inquisitive as to how I was coping. A little embarrassed, I pulled my nightshirt over my breasts.

"I'm getting nothing. It seems like a pointless exercise," I said, reaching for the tiny fingers of little Jessica's as she lay quietly with her eyes shut in what looked like a Perspex cot.

"You've got to keep trying. It takes about three days for your milk to come in. You will first produce colostrums, this is very good for your baby, it's high in nutrients and helps prevent infection," the nurse said as she took the pump away. "I'll bring you the pump every three hours and let's see how long it takes for your milk to come in." She left the room.

I was alone with my daughter. It felt strange yet wonderful. Her body, so little weighing just over 2 kilograms at birth, seemed too fragile to hold. I motioned to the edge of the bed and propped myself up so I could lean over the Perspex cot and pick her up, so that she could lie on my chest. In her nose she had a tube, the tube by which she was being fed. And despite her minute size, she certainly had loads of hair.

Jessica, you don't take after your father luckily!

As Benjamin walked into the room, I was quietly sitting holding Jessica while she slept. Benjamin carried two bags with him and two tied bunches of flowers.

"I picked these up on my way in. Thought they'd cheer you up and brighten the room. Have you called anyone yet?" Benjamin asked as he gently took Jessica from me.

"No, I've been waiting for you."

"Well let's get going, we've quite a few calls to make." Benjamin handed me the mobile phone.

We called our respective families and close friends and told them the news. It was a wonderful surprise to all except my mother, who having spoken to me on the Monday night, the day my waters actually broke, had already suspected the birth was imminent. She later told me of the dream she had had the night of my delivery.

"Do you need me to come?" Mum asked. She had planned to join me three weeks after the babies were born.

"No, it's no point yet Mum. I'm still in hospital and will be for at least a week. Jessica is here with me and William is in the Special Care Baby Unit. I will need you once they're out, Mum," thinking that this ordeal would only last a week or two.

"Emma, before you hang up, sweetheart, I've got some sad news to tell you." As Mum said this, I looked across at Benjamin and motioned to him to come over and stand by my bedside.

Chapter Ten

As I sit now at my desk, recollecting, I can't believe that a year's passed since that symbolic day at St Mary's Hospital. That early February morning, the very same morning I gave birth to Jessica and William, two incredible miracles in my life. Such momentous change, so many tumultuous events happened this past year. I am sad to be saying goodbye as I finish my letter to Aunt Viv and close the book on that chapter of my life, yet at the same time I'm filled with anticipation for the future Benjamin and I will share with our two precious children.

Dear Viv,

We now have two new additions to the family, Jessica and William Hogan.

Oh, how I wish you were here!

The birth itself was a breeze, once I'd had the epidural you could have cut me in half and I'd have been none the wiser. I've been caught off guard though, it all happened so fast. I have to catch myself looking at my tummy trying to remember they're out! It doesn't look like it though, I'm still eighteen kilos heavier than I was at our last visit together and, what's worse I have an added layer of skin loosely flapping just above my fanny line, just in case I get cold. Don't tell anyone but I don't feel quite as excited as I should. I've dreamed of this moment for ages and pictured my baby suckling from my breast, sleeping soundly, chubby cheeked and all. Instead I'm frightened as all hell and I'm completely bewildered.

No need to panic though I'll pull through, you know I will.

You've always been my confidant, my stalwart and although you can't be here with me now, I'll keep you in the picture through my letters. I've decided to write to you to tell you all our news as the story unfolds. At least I'll try for as long as I have the time. I'm on maternity leave for six months so I'll need something to keep me busy.

Hugs and kisses
Emma-Beez

Benjamin stayed late that night after sitting beside William's incubator for an hour and a half before coming to see Jessica and I. His face was pale and his eyes sunken. He had a long drive home and I was concerned that he might fall asleep at the wheel.

"Don't you think you should head home, sweetheart?"
"I'm fine. I'll stay a while with you and Jessica until she goes to the nursery. Have you tried her on the breast again?"

"Yes, but firstly there's very little milk right now and secondly she gets so tired," I confessed.

"You don't have to breast-feed you know. Don't put pressure on yourself." Benjamin pointed out the alternative I hadn't contemplated yet.

"I know but I'll feel like I've let them down. They need my milk even more being premature."

I was given a sleeping pill that evening after persevering every three to four hours to encourage my milk to come in. It seemed abnormal. I should have had two bouncy babies suckling from my breast instead I had to improvise and use this damned pump! By nine thirty that evening I had produced over forty millilitres of colostrum per breast. The nurses were amazed at how quickly I had produced such quantities of colostrum. Well, the blue veins all over my breasts had to be indicating something.

I woke the next morning feeling a little stronger and dying to see my little William. I spent quite a bit of time with Jessica in the early hours of the morning. We hadn't tried to get her to latch again. I felt it was too much for her; having to deal with the real world was enough, she'd learn how to breast-feed in her own time. In the meantime, I became a dedicated four hourly breast pump expert. The nurses would save a little colostrum for Jessica and keep it in the Lindo Wing while the rest would be sent across the way to the Neonatal Unit for William. Although I hadn't seen him yet and both babies were so little, I felt that the colostrum and eventually my milk, when it came in, were helping them to fight and get stronger.

I waited for Benjamin to come with me to the Neonatal Unit to see William for the first time since the birth. I knew that I couldn't handle this first visit on my own. As it was, Benjamin had called into the office and was taking the rest of the week off.

"Are you ready?" Benjamin squeezed my hand as he pushed me in the wheelchair through the maize of underground passages to the other side of the hospital where the Neonatal Unit was.

"I'm nervous. I don't know what to expect," I said, hands shaking a little.

"Just be calm and be strong, he will know who you are and he needs you to be resilient." Benjamin touched my shoulder as he pushed the elevator button.

I was to get to know this route so well over the next seven days that I could have travelled it blindfolded.

We reached the third floor and made our way down the passage toward the Neonatal Unit. There was a security buzzer on the door, so we waited for someone to answer.

"Can I help you?" the voice through the intercom said.

I could see nurses and what must be parents walking around through the glass portion of the door. It was a hive of activity.

"Yes, it is Mr And Mrs Hogan here to see our son William Hogan in the Intensive Care Unit," Benjamin said.

"Oh yes. Good news they've moved him overnight to the High Care Unit. Come in," the voice said, as the buzzer sounded and we pushed the door open.

I was suddenly conscious that I wasn't dressed. I was in my nightshirt and dressing gown as I couldn't shower yet and I was unable to walk on my own. I felt self-conscious and insecure, at the mercy of those doctors not only because I was recovering from major surgery but because my baby, William was under their care.

The sister took us past two incubators. She pointed out to us where little, tiny William lay and then left us to experience this reunion for ourselves.

Benjamin let go of my hand as I walked quietly over to see my little baby boy. There in this minuscule crib lay William, totally naked except for a grotesque looking knitted hat on his tiny head. Nothing prepared me for how small he was, nothing!

Machines surrounded him and it seemed as if he had a hundred tubes attached to every inch of his body from his head, to his nose, to his heart, to his lungs to his feet. I felt as if I had left this world as I knew it, and I had entered the world of science fiction.

As I lent over the crib to lift my baby boy up into my arms and hold him for the first time, I couldn't but help think how all this high tech equipment dwarfed him. How intimidating it must be for one so premature, so fragile, to be out in this big world.

My maternal instincts took over and my heart beat twice as fast as I brought him to my chest, as I put my arms ever so gently around him and held him so he could enjoy the warmth of my body and hear the beating of my heart: the few things he was used to while inside my womb; things that would be familiar to him and would bring him some form of comfort. I needed him to feel that I was his home that I was here now and he would be safe.

I sat there with William, my eyes closed praying he'd be fine, when I was interrupted by the presence of a stranger. A woman in her mid forties came up to William and I and peered at me on bended knee.

I was so taken aback that I was at a loss for words.

"Are you Mrs Hogan?" she asked.

"Yes, why?" I asked.

"This is your first meeting with your son, William, I believe?" she asked another question. Where was this leading to and who was she?

"May I ask who you are and what your role is?" I asked, somewhat indignant.

"I'm the family counsellor and was wondering if I could ask you a few questions?" Hadn't she asked me enough already for one morning. How inappropriate her timing was.

"This is a sacred time for me with my son, would you mind giving us some space," I said, tears welling in my eyes.

I think she finally got the hint and slowly backed away, leaving a little note beside the chair I was sitting in.

"I am usually in the family lounge situated to the right of the corridor just before you enter the Neonatal Unit. If you and your husband ever need someone to talk to please feel free to call on me. There is tea and coffee and a television in the family room, so you can spend some time away from the ward," she added, as she moved out of the room greeting Benjamin on the way out.

"Do you know her?" I asked Benjamin.

"Well sort of. She was here last night and wanted to see you. I said you'd be here today." That explained the somewhat obtrusive invasion of our privacy.

Benjamin and I spent two hours with William before I was introduced to the nursing staff and two of the four consultant paediatricians in the unit. The differences between the Intensive Care, High Care and Special Care Units were explained to us and I understood a little more about the equipment before I left to get back to my hospital bed and my dreaded breast pump.

Viv Darling,

I saw William today. You couldn't imagine how miniature he is, not even the dolls clothes you used to make for my doll would fit him. He's in High Care now. How can I explain it to you so you'll understand what it's like in there?

Well, you remember those chicks I had when I was eight? It's like the incubator they were in until they'd hatched and grown a little. Bright lights and as hot as the Kalahari Desert. He's not on oxygen any more but there are hundreds of tubes attached to his every orifice and then some. The nurses are feeding him my expressed breast milk.

Now there's a thing. With your boobs you'd have made a terrific jersey cow yourself, but believe it or not, nature has a way of taking care of its own. In spite of my ordinarily small breasts, I've tons of milk; in fact they've nicknamed me after the bovine species. I might donate some to the milk bank for babies whose mothers have HIV AIDS. I'm taking a sleeping pill at night to help me stay asleep. I know don't tell me, you've never liked pills but I really do need them right now, if you saw my face and looked into my eyes you'd know how stressed I am. You'd probably prescribe the whole bottle!

Take care,
Emma-Beez

Back in my hospital bed, Benjamin and I spent a little time with Jessica and while I pumped milk Benjamin stroked her head.

"I feel such a fool. Like I'm using a vacuum cleaner for some obscene sexual pleasure!" I said jokingly.

"I know. I must admit it does look quite strange, but hey you're giving them your antibodies," Benjamin giggled.

In the meantime people had sent dozens of flowers to the hospital, my room looked like a florist. Both my work and Benjamin's had sent the most exquisite bunch of flowers which took up half the space in the little room. The rest of the flowers, which couldn't fit in my room, I had given to the nurses, which they placed all around the Lindo Wing. Everywhere you looked there was a bowl of flowers. I felt sorry for anyone who might have suffered from hay fever.

Susan and John, Phoebe and Richard, Bianca and Ross, Sophie and Steve had all called Benjamin to say they were dying to come and see the twins.

"Darling, I'm not ready to see anyone yet. I will break down into tears and be unable to talk about the birth and about the twins. Just give me a few more days, please." I felt fragile, vulnerable and a failure that my babies were born so soon and so small. I wasn't ready for all the questions I'd be asked. I just needed a little time to come to terms with everything that had happened and was happening to me, to us.

"Emma, I understand. They are only being supportive and want to share your joy with you to help you through the pain, that's all," Benjamin said.

"What time are you planning on travelling back home?" He was commuting into the City every morning to be with his family, while in the evenings he had to travel back to an empty house on his own.

"It's funny Emma, I have a family of four now, but at night, lying in bed on my own, I feel the loneliest I've ever felt," Benjamin confessed.

"Benjamin, I'm sorry it's not going to be easy for a while. I'll be home soon though, then we will be together at least," I said, in a weak effort to try and console him.

We both knew in our hearts though that this would be just the beginning of what we later found out would be one of the most stressful periods in our relationship. No one could have prepared us for the degree of exhaustion or the constant anxiety we would suffer in the weeks and months to come.

Chapter Eleven

Three sisters walked into my room and turning the lights on low, woke me in the middle of the night.

"What's the matter?" I asked, panic in my voice as I sat bolt upright in my bed.

"Don't panic Mrs Hogan, but we have some news for you about Jessica." As the nurse said this I burst into tears fearing the worst of my nightmares had come true.

"Where is she?" I demanded.

"She is safe now. She stopped breathing a half hour ago. I was on duty and I had tucked her in under her covers. She had just had her last feed when I heard her cough twice and then there was silence. Concerned I turned back to see how she was doing and found her body had begun to turn blue, she had stopped breathing. Fortunately, Lucy was nearby and she called the Neonatal Unit while I tried to resuscitate her. By the time the Neonatal Unit had arrived, literally two minutes after the call, Jessica was breathing again." The sister was also in tears. She had obviously got the fright of her life.

"Oh Thank God," was all I could say. Someone had looked after her that night and had saved her life. I felt sick to the bone.

"We didn't notify you earlier as there wasn't time, we needed to get her breathing again. I'm sorry," she added apologetically.

"Where is she now?" I asked.

"She's with her brother in the Neonatal Unit. They have her in Intensive Care to monitor her and will be doing a few tests to make sure everything is fine," she said.

"May I see her?"

"Yes, but I suggest you wait until a little later, until seven o'clock perhaps. Let the doctors there run the various test so that by the time you get there they can inform you about the results. There's nothing you can do, Jessica was asleep when I left her five minutes ago." She had gone with Jessica and the Neonatal staff to the unit.

I was in a state of shock. Just as William seemed to be getting stronger this happened.

"She wanted to be with her brother, I think," I said to the nurse, as she got up from the chair she had been sitting in to leave.

"Will you arrange for the porter to take me across to the Neonatal Unit at seven o'clock?" I asked.

"Yes, of course." She closed the door behind her. I immediately picked up the phone to call Benjamin without looking at the clock to see what time it was.

"What's the matter Emma?" Benjamin said in a sleepy yet stressed voice. "Do you know what time it is?" he asked.

"No," I said.

"It's four o'clock in the morning," he said.

"I'm sorry." I burst into tears again. "It's Jessica," I said, and then stopped to catch my breath.

"Where is she?" Benjamin asked.

"She stopped breathing about an hour ago and they took her to the Neonatal Unit after managing to resuscitate her here," I said. "She's with William now but in the Intensive Care Unit, in an incubator being monitored."

"I'll get dressed and I'll be with you as soon as I can." Poor Benjamin, he had been pushed into the deep end of fatherhood without really knowing it.

"She's stable now, no need to panic the worst of it is over and she's going to be fine they say," I said, and replaced the receiver.

At seven o'clock the porter came to collect me in the wheelchair. As he pushed me along the dark, narrow passageway to the other side of the hospital, I wondered what it would have been like to have a single full term baby. Would or even could my friends and family comprehend what it was like to have two premature babies both in hospital. The unexplainable joy of having had Jessica and William was overshadowed by the challenges they now faced to stay alive and to thrive.

The very basic functions, like breathing, eating, swallowing, regulating their temperature their heart rate, were all huge challenges for them everyday where for healthy full term babies these came naturally. Instead of spending their energies on learning how to survive in the world, healthy full term babies begin to thrive almost from the very moment they are born.

I hadn't been into the Intensive Care Unit before that morning. They only really allowed parents into the unit. I learnt quickly how protective you become of your premature infant and how important privacy for the parents is. Things like peering into another baby's crib and asking questions about another baby's well being, were not tolerated by parents or staff within the unit. For many reasons not least of which were the risk of infection and out of respect for the parent's right to confidentiality.

As I walked into the Intensive Care Unit, I felt overwhelmed by the equipment and the thought of how dehumanising it all appeared to be. There were babies as young as twenty-four and twenty-six weeks' gestation fighting desperately for survival in their oversized incubators. Their body organs barely developed, the risk of infection being so great that some parents were only allowed to hold their baby's tiny fingers through a peephole in the incubator. Some would suffer hearing problems, sight problems, breathing or heart related problems and others even brain damage for the rest of their lives. I wondered what had given us the right to play God and keep a foetus alive in an artificially created environment, a microcosm of the womb? At what costs had we advanced our medicinal capabilities?

But then on the other hand, this very same equipment was helping my own babies to complete their development outside the womb. As a mother I didn't care about intellectual debates, all I cared about right now was the survival of my children no matter how young or fragile.

Jessica lay sound asleep in her incubator under the warmth of lights, hooked up to two different machines. The doctors had told me that they had run all sorts of tests and all had come back negative.

"What happened then?" I asked bewildered.

"It can happen, she probably needed some extra support and this was her way of telling us," the paediatrician said, as he ran through the tests they had done on Jessica during the past six hours.

"What do you do now?" I asked again.

"Well, we will keep her here for another two hours or so and make sure that she continues to be stable, at which point we will move her to the Special Care Unit to be with her brother. She's lost a little more weight so we will watch this closely. But there's no sign of infection, thank goodness," he said.

They had moved William out of High Care and into Special Care as he was no longer jaundiced and his weight had picked up a little.

This was a roller coaster ride and I couldn't seem to get off it.

"Mandy here, has been assigned to Jessica for today so she will be able to answer any further questions you might have." Each baby in the Intensive Care Unit was assigned a dedicated and highly trained member of staff, unlike the High Care and Special Care Units where there were three babies per staff member.

"Mrs Hogan there's someone at the door waiting to see you." A nurse had entered the room behind without me hearing her.

"Thank you. Where is she waiting?" I asked. As I turned around I saw Phoebe standing in the doorway of the Intensive Care Unit.

"Oh Phoebe you couldn't have come at a better time," I said. "How did you know?" I asked.

"Benjamin called me and asked if I could come down to see you, he is running late, work called and needed him for a few hours." Phoebe walked over to me and gave me a huge hug. It was Benjamin's financial year-end and it was the most crucial time in his calendar year. Although he'd taken paternity leave, he'd said if they needed him, they shouldn't hesitate to call him in. Which they had obviously done!

I just held on to her tightly as she whispered in my ear.

"You will be fine, Jessica and William will be fine, you'll see."

"It's been so hard Phoebe. It's not what I had expected," I said.

"It never is my friend. It never quite is," she said quietly. "So explain to me what all this incredibly high tech equipment is all about?" Phoebe and I spent an hour talking about the delivery, the Neonatal Unit, the twins, breast-feeding or lack of and expressing. I felt a whole lot better afterwards as if a ton of stone had been lifted from my shoulders and I didn't have to bear the load alone anymore.

Phoebe stayed a little longer but had been told she was only allowed to be in the unit for a half hour, being a visitor and not a parent, so she felt she should leave before she got in anyone's way.

"Benjamin will be with you shortly, I'm sure. You must be strong for the sake of your babies Emma," Phoebe said as she and I kissed each other goodbye.

I informed Mandy that I was going to see how William was doing in Special Care and she could call me if she felt Jessica needed me.

William was also asleep, tucked in under layers of blankets to help keep him warm. I don't quiet know how anyone, even a little premature baby could possibly get cold in that hot house! It was unbearably hot. I'm convinced now that the extreme heat was one of the reasons I often became so emotional and felt so out of control, in the early weeks of being in the unit, or that was my explanation to Benjamin at least.

I was watching two mums top and tail their babies and then change them. It was amazing how they managed with such confidence and skilfulness to negotiate the many tubes and to console their hysterical infants during the process. Each baby had its own consol as such in which there was a stash of nappies, cotton wool, a top and tail bowl, bum cream, dummies, sterilising solution and anything else that specific infant required. There were seven babies in Special Care and each at different stages of development and progress.

"I'm Roxanne. Is that your son over there?" One of the mums I had been watching came over and spoke to me.

"Yes, his name is William, he's a twin. His sister Jessica will be joining him soon, she's had a blip and is in the Intensive Care Unit right now," I said openly.

"We've all been there. It will get better." The other mum, a mum of twins also, came up to the two of us. "My name is Nbeni and I have twins. Two little girls. They were born at twenty-nine weeks," she said.

"I can't believe how confident you are around your babies. It seems so difficult and I'm so nervous," I said.

"So was I to begin with, but you get used to their size and when you see a big chunky full term baby come in, you can't believe how large they are," Nbeni said.

"Do you know your way around?" Roxanne asked.

"No, not really," I said.

"Well, Nbeni and I can give you a quick and dirty guided tour," Roxanne said as she took my hand, and she and Nbeni explained how things worked in the unit and where I could find clothes to change William. They showed me where the supply of nappies, cotton wool and bum cream were kept. They pointed out to me where the new linen for the cribs was. Last but not least they introduced me to Lillian one of the two nurses on duty.

"Hi I'm Lillian, I've been looking after William today," she said.

"Thank you. You sound Australian, where are you from?" I said.

"Yes, I'm Australian, my husband and I are living in the United Kingdom for a few years and then plan to return," Lillian said.

"Are you a permanent staff member here?" I asked knowing that most of the nursing staff like the paediatricians were consultants and charged a far higher rate than any permanent staff member would.

"No, I'm a consultant," Lillian said. "I am trying to sort out a space and another crib in here for Jessica, your daughter. I believe she's joining us today."

"Yes. I think it will be better for them to be together," I said, relieved that someone so nice was taking care of my babies. "How long are your hours?"

"We work twelve hour shifts. I usually only work the day shift and am usually here on Tuesdays, Wednesdays and Thursdays," she said.

I immediately warmed to her. Lillian appeared really competent and I trusted her instinctively.

"I will show you how I prepare William's feed so that you can feed him soon," Lillian suggested.

"I'll watch for now I think. I'm petrified I'll stick the tube down his wind pipe or something," I confessed.

Just then the bleeper of his machine went off. I got such a fright and ran to his crib.

"What's the matter?" I asked Lillian when the monitor had stopped bleeping and she had checked William and jiggled his toes.

"He just had an apnoea attack, where he stopped breathing for a while and his heart rate also fell below one hundred as a result," she said, as she recorded this incident in his little black book by his crib.

Every time William or Jessica's monitors went off, it was as if my heart also stopped beating for a moment and my breathing paused. This became one of the hardest things to get used to, especially after the close encounter with Jessica.

Just then Benjamin walked into the room.

"Excuse me for a moment Lillian, that's my husband," I said and ran over to him.

"I was so frightened for Jessica. But they say she's stable now."

"Yes I know, I've spent the last twenty minutes talking to the paediatrician in Intensive Care," Benjamin said as he hugged me. "She's where she needs to be now for a while. It was her way of telling us, Emma."

"This is Lillian. She's looking after William today," I said as we walked over to Lillian. "Please continue with your explanation of what an apnoea attack is."

"Pleased to meet you Mr Hogan," Lillian said. "Mrs Hogan…"

"Please call me Emma."

"Thanks. Emma, you'll get used to the monitors. It's common for premature infants to stop breathing; actually even full term infants stop breathing but only for short periods of around five seconds before they're able to restart breathing themselves. The premature infant can't restart on his or her own, that's why we prompt them or remind them by jiggling their feet," she explained, as she went over to the counter on the other side of the room and picked up a book.

"Here, take this for a few days and read it. It'll help you understand a little more about it all," Lillian said as she handed me the book she had picked up, *Your Premature Baby* by Nikki Bradford.

"We're giving William caffeine which will help both his breathing as well as his heart rate," Lillian said as she added his medication to his feed in the syringe.

"Won't this make him irritable and hyperactive?" I asked, imagining that if caffeine helped to stimulate adults and get them going in the mornings it must certainly have some sort of negative effect on a baby.

"If he starts to climb out of his crib, then we know he's had too much," Lillian said jokingly.

"Lillian, may I ask you a question?" Benjamin asked.

"Yes, sure," she said.

"Emma and I were wondering why the hospital didn't bring Jessica into the Neonatal Unit straight away?"

"It is difficult to answer, but there could have been a number of reasons, some good some not so good." Lillian obviously knew the system well.

"Go on," Benjamin said.

"First, hospitals in general like to keep the babies with their mothers wherever possible. Where this isn't possible and the baby requires more specialised care and attention, the baby is taken to a neonatal ward not always at the same hospital, depending on the availability of beds and staff."

"Do you mean they would move the baby to another hospital even if this was further away from the parents home?" I asked.

"Yes."

"As you can imagine, the National Health System is under a lot of pressure, too many requests and not enough qualified staff, cots or money to cater for all of them. The Neonatal Units around the country, and this is one of the best, have to keep a tight budget each year. It's all about priorities. If a premature baby appears strong and their APGAR score is high then a baby with more severe problems will be given priority," Lillian said.

I was later to learn a whole lot more about the NHS and would also come to understand, from personal experience, just how unfair these systems could be.

Hi Viv,

February 2003

My new nickname as of yesterday is Jersey Cow and I'm fast becoming the connoisseur of milk production. I'm forever leaking like a dripping tap whose seal has gone. Benjamin can't go near my boobs for fear of drowning in milk so foreplay has become quite limited really. I think I'm keeping both the breast pad industry as well as the bottle company for frozen breast milk in business. I seem to have already filled the two allocated drawers in the hospital freezer with milk so I'm taking milk home now. Benjamin's not impressed. I'm hijacking the space usually reserved especially for his Magnum ice creams.

On a more serious note, Jessica stopped breathing on us the other day and was taken to ICU. I think she was jealous of all the attention William was getting and felt left out! Don't fret she'll be fine. I'm not so sure about me though.

I met some of the other mums today. They're amazing with their preemies. They seem to manage so well with their little drowned rats as I call them, screaming, naked and ever so tiny. I just don't seem to be able to get it right; I've got butterfingers for the first time Viv. I'm usually quite good with my hands as you know with all the ball sports you used to watch me play, but this is a different league all together.

William won't take my boob, he just screams blue murder every time I put him anywhere near them. I know my nipples are the size of avocado pips but hey he's going to have to like boobs and nipples some day why not get the hang of them now?

There's never a dull moment. Wish you could see them.
Hugs and kisses
Emma-Beez

I had tried to breast-feed William every day since he had moved into the Special Care Unit, but he just seemed to hate the breast more, the harder I tried. The breast-feeding expert, who I later found out had never had children herself, tried incessantly to get William to latch. I felt as if it was mandatory that my babies breast-fed and that there was no alternative. I could have understood the fixation with breast-feeding had I been living in the deepest darkest part of Africa where there was nothing other than my bare naked boobs to feed my children, but I wasn't. There was an alternative and it didn't even entail sacrificing the goodness of breast milk: it was feeding William my breast milk by bottle.

"Emma, I must encourage you to persevere with William, as he starts to feed himself you must give him your boob first. If he sucks on a teat he'll never take the boob. It's the easier option for him." The breast-feeding-expert-with-no-children kept saying to me.

Anyway, I wasn't going to get too upset about it just now as both Jessica and William were still predominantly being fed by tube, as they got too tired to take a full feed on the breast or by bottle.

I travelled into the hospital from Surrey daily leaving home at the crack of dawn and returning late at night with Benjamin. Benjamin would commute from work changing tubes three times to get from Bank to Paddington and then he would walk from the station to St Mary's Hospital. It was a commuter's nightmare and it took everything we had to keep our spirits up. I found myself falling asleep on the morning train into the City and often was woken by one of the train stewards cleaning up, having been stationary at Waterloo already for as long as ten minutes. I felt physically and mentally drained. I was not only dealing with being a mother of two but also a mother of two premature babies still in hospital. I was also getting little sleep since I continued to express day and night, every four hours. I knew that my babies, once home, would need more milk and I had to keep up the supply.

Benjamin and I didn't let on to the hospital how difficult the commute really was as they had hinted a number of times that they had tried to see if St Peters or the Royal Surrey had space to take our babies on. We didn't want the hospital to have an excuse to move the babies. I certainly felt strongly about them staying put. I had chosen St Mary's when we were living in Kensington and had chosen it for a reason. The reason being that if I needed any extra care or the babies, it was readily available and we wouldn't have to be moved. St Mary's also had one of the very best Neonatal Units in the country. I didn't want to disturb my babies' progress and I believed by moving them, we would set them back.

"Emma." Lillian called me aside one morning while I was watching over William and Jessica.

"Yes, what is it?" I said, as I got up from my chair beside the twins' cribs and walked over to where Lillian was standing.

"Do you have a moment?" she said quietly.

"Sure. Shall we take a walk outside the unit?" I asked, knowing that the other nurse on duty could watch the babies for ten minutes.

"Emma, I thought I'd mention something to you which came up in a meeting I had with the management team of the unit yesterday. I want to tell you because I disagreed with their decision and told them so during the meeting." My heart sank. I knew they were trying to get my babies out of the unit and they had probably found space at a hospital elsewhere.

"What's going on?"

"The paediatricians asked me yesterday during my status report if I thought the Hogan twins were ready to be discharged." She paused as she saw my face turn pale with worry. "I showed them the records and took them through the past week's progress of each baby. It is clearly obvious that they are not ready. They are still experiencing too many apnoeas, meaning a cessation of airflow during sleep and bradycardias, meaning slow heart rate or rhythm and they are still on the monitors. My recommendation was a definite no, but I'm not sure what their final decision will be." Lillian's news hit me like a ton of lead. I couldn't understand why they couldn't just let my babies get strong and healthy? Why couldn't they just leave them be like all the other babies in the unit, to progress in their own time at their own pace? Why were they pushing them? All they needed was time.

"Lillian, how can they discharge them? They're still being tube fed with an occasional breast or bottle when they are able. They're also still on Ranitidine for their reflux," I protested.

"I know you don't want to hear this but they are taking the babies off the monitors in two days' time if their apnoeas and bradycardias decrease, and they have sent babies home in the past on nasal gastric tubes," Lillian said.

"Lillian if there's one thing you'll get to know about me that's determination. They will not move my babies and they will not discharge them until I say they're ready," I said adamantly.

"We need to buy you some time then Emma," Lillian said, plotting in her mind how we'd accomplish that.

"Keep a record of all the apnoeas and bradycardias even if you would not usually record them. That way the record will speak for itself as an objective voice," I said, and felt as if a judge and jury were trying me. I would give my babies as much time as they needed even if it meant stealing that time.

"Lillian they're not even thirty-eight weeks yet. It's absurd!"

That evening I told Benjamin about the incident and after a little thought he said:

"Emma, I've been thinking about this hidden agenda of theirs. I think I know why," he said as he switched the television off.

"Why?"

"First, think about what keeps the hospital and any for that matter alive outside of government funds." He paused and then continued.

"It's all about money, about reputation and about statistics. A unit like the one at St Mary's needs additional outside funding to afford the experienced staff, the high tech equipment and more. One avenue to secure funding is to build an outstanding reputation for nursing premature babies, especially those as young as twenty-four and twenty-six weeks gestation or infants with other types of serious conditions. They can only take on premature babies into

Intensive Care if they can move the healthier ones into High Care and again those from High Care into Special Care. Those in Special Care are being prepared for home, so it's important that once there are signs that they are progressing and if there's pressure to take on new babies into Intensive Care, that they are discharged. These units have budgets, which they need to work within, and they have incentives to come under budget every year. Our babies are not unique or extra special, at the end of the day they're just a number and are subject to the system. The bottom line is that our babies are becoming stronger and now could be seen as taking up space and budget, both of which could be spent on more critical cases," he said.

"Do you think the fact that we moved from Kensington to Surrey has anything to do with it?"

"Yes I do. We no longer technically fall under their jurisdiction and we should be using up the budget of a Surrey hospital," Benjamin said. "That's putting it crudely."

"I hear what you're saying, but it doesn't make it any easier. These are my babies and I'll do everything in my power to buy time until they're ready to leave," I said.

"That's fine Emma, but play it cool and respect their priorities," Benjamin advised.

"I also think I'm going to ask Mum to come earlier. I think I need her. Do you mind?"

"If she can get away and is available to come sooner, of course I don't mind," Benjamin said.

Benjamin is the type of person who doesn't like houseguests for too long. They tend to cramp his style a bit. So I'd always tried to make sure Mum and Dad never stayed too long, but perhaps this time would have to be an exception. Mum would probably be with us for three weeks and anyway it was about time Benjamin got used to people and chaos, once the babies were home life would never be the same again.

"Hi Mum. How are you?"

"I'm fine. How are Jessica and William doing today?"

"They're getting on slowly. William still suffers quite a few apnoeas and is not yet able to take a full bottle-feed. Jessica is getting stronger after her scare. She is off the caffeine and Ranitidine and her apnoeas are almost gone. I'm managing to breast-feed her three times a day, she is then too tired to manage any more and we tube feed her in between," I said

"Did they have their hearing tests yet?"

"Yes and Jessica passed in both ears while William failed in his right ear. They'll have to re-test in three months' time again." I had been worried about William's test results but in the greater scheme of things I knew that this was not the worst of our worries. I had to help the babies to self-feed and to stabilise their heart rates and breathing. These were critical in order for them to come home. The paediatricians had said that William might have had fluid on his ear or the test might have been done a little too early at thirty-six weeks gestation. I didn't have the energy, if I was honest with myself, to panic about just one more blip.

"They were going to take them off the monitors yesterday, but they've been suffering too many apnoeas still, so they will leave them for a couple more days thank goodness," I said.

"Why don't you want them off the machines?" she asked.

"If they are off the machines they can technically come home even if they are still being fed mainly by tube. I'm not prepared to feed my babies by tube at home and I'm frightened that they're pushing them too quickly, a little like taking a cake out of the oven too soon: it looks ready from afar but after a few minutes outside the oven it will begin to flop," I said. "I'm also concerned that their breathing isn't yet stable and without the machines to prove this I'm at the hospital's mercy."

"Mum, the reason I actually called was to ask you if you can do something for me," I said tentatively.

"Sure, what do you need?"

"Can you come over as soon as possible?" I knew my parents had plans, which they would have to cancel.

"Are you sure I won't be in the way, especially in Benjamin's way. I know how he is with houseguests?" Mum and Dad had stayed with us over Christmas for three weeks to help us move into our new home. It turned out to be just a little too long and Benjamin eventually got irritable and impatient, which became awkward for me.

"No, I've spoken to him and said that I need you here," I said.

"I'll have to see what I can do. Dad and I had plans and I need to see if I can get on another flight at such short notice. I'll let you know." Mum was already planning in her head how she was going to arrange everything.

One thing for certain, she was a devoted mother and when any one of her children called for help, she'd always be there.

"I need you. The hospital is playing a tough game and keeps trying to move the babies to another hospital or release them too early. I'm fighting them the best I can and trying to buy time, but it would be good to have a friend, Mum."

I could sense that this request had moved her to tears and it pulled at her own heartstrings. I knew then that she would come straight away regardless of the cost.

"I'll call you tomorrow. I love you," she said as she sniffed and then replaced the receiver.

Viv,

I'm not as strong as I thought I was Viv. You often said people who appear in total control are often not really enjoying life's spontaneity. Well if that's the case my cup runneth over. I think you're not the only one losing their mind. I now understand what you meant when you said this to me in South Africa. I called Mum today and asked her to come over as soon as possible. I need a woman in the house.

I'm not saying that Benjamin's not any good, but he's too calm and unemotional. I know Mum will cry with me, she'll smile with me and she'll lose her cool with me. That's how we woman are.

I think the hospital are conspiring against the Hogan twins and are trying to get rid of my babies as soon as possible. There are two critically ill babies waiting to be transferred to the hospital right now and those are only the ones I know about, there could be many more. Benjamin says, unsympathetically, I'm reading too much into it and that if anything it's all about budgets, priorities and resources, but the bottom line for me is I don't give a shit. They're staying put until they're ready to come home and not a day too soon. Oops, I know, my swearing has worsened lately.

It will be interesting to see Mum's reaction when she sees the twins; they're not what you'd expect. I've enclosed two photos of the babies for you.

Take care, I'll write again soon.

Emma-Beez

"Mrs Hogan, there are going to be some visiting students later today, would you mind answering a few questions for them?" one of the other nurses asked as Lillian was off duty today.

"What sort of questions?" I asked apprehensively.

"They are doing research around premature infants and would like to ask you a few questions about your experience," the nurse said.

"Emma, I'm going to participate if that's any help." Roxanne, who had overheard the conversation, added from across the room.

I felt as if I would be letting the side down if I didn't and agreed to it.

I was sitting peacefully with Jessica in my arms breast-feeding, when the breast-feeding-expert-with-no-children came up to me totally unexpectedly. Damn, I thought, how invasive. I couldn't even breast-feed in peace without someone interrupting me! I tried to hide the flesh of my boobs and remain calm so as not to disturb Jessica, but it didn't work. Jessica let go of my nipple and oops my entire boob was exposed! Darn it.

"Yes," I said rather irritated.

"Have you tried William on the breast again?"

Why couldn't she just leave the subject well and truly alone? Did she have a hidden agenda? Was she earning a bonus based on the number of woman in the unit she could convince to breast-feed? There must have been some logical explanation.

"Do you ever give up?" I asked as jokingly as I could.

"No," she said bluntly.

"Well, to tell you the honest truth I haven't. The last time I tried was three nights ago. He just did the same thing. He yelled and yelled until he went blue in the face and only stopped once I had taken the boob away from him," I said.

"May I help you?" she persisted.

"Look. What's so wrong with giving him my breast milk in a bottle if he's happy?" I asked now quite irritated. They all seemed to make everything their business.

"Don't you feel as if you have bonded really well with Jessica?" she asked.

"Yes I do." I did feel closer to Jessica than to William but I wasn't sure if this had anything to do with the fact that I was breast-feeding her and not him.

"I think you'd feel a whole lot closer to William if you put him to your breast," she urged. Was she looking at it from my point of view or William's and was she more concerned with my state of mind than his well being?

"You're probably right, but I can't even get him to look at my breast without panicking and bursting into tears. There must be a reason why he doesn't want to latch. It upsets me more to force him and to see him in such a state," I said.

171

"Well, it's your choice but the longer you give him the bottle the less chance there is of him ever breast-feeding." Was she finally stepping down?

"I know all this. If you ask me I think he was born so small and too soon. He simply doesn't know what to do. The breast intimidates him," I said, and continued to try to get Jessica back onto my boob to finish her feed. By this stage she had lost interest completely and was fast asleep.

I had learnt with premature babies you have a window of opportunity to get them to suckle and if you miss that wake time then it's no use trying. Jessica, although she could breast-feed, tired very easily, and the effort was often just too great for her.

Later that afternoon as I was reading a book waiting for Jessica's next feed and to feed William by tube, something Lillian had taught me how to do. Three students approached me from the far side of the ward.

"I thought there was going to be only one person interviewing me," I said, surprised by how many people there now were in the unit and the level of noise.

"Yes, we know. Do you mind if we all interview you?" one student asked.

"Yes I do. I think they're too many people for a start in the unit. You'll disturb the babies in here and I also think I can only cope with one set of questions," I said honestly but bluntly.

"We understand. I'll be the one to ask you some questions," the oldest looking student said as the others left the room. I'm sure they were thinking what a cow!

I suddenly felt like a goldfish in a glass bowl where everyone seemed to know my business and nothing remained confidential. Another student had approached Roxanne and she winked at me from across the room. Her gesture made me relax a little.

"How old are your twins?" she asked.

"Just over thirty-six weeks' gestation. They were born at thirty-four weeks," I said.

"Can you tell me a little about their birth and the first few days in hospital?" she went on.

"I had an emergency c-section as my waters broke twenty-four hours before we arrived at the hospital. I also had an epidural and was in theatre for two hours. Jessica came to the Lindo Wing with me straight away while William was taken to the Intensive Care Unit," I said.

"How much did your babies weigh?"

"Jessica weighed two point zero five kilos and William weighed one point eight kilos."

"Did either Jessica or William require oxygen?" she asked.

"William was put on CPAP for twelve hours while Jessica was fine until she stopped breathing and needed resuscitating two days later and was brought to SCBU."

"Sorry, that's the Special Care Baby Unit, is that correct?"

"Yes, the Intensive Care ward. William also suffered jaundice for a week or so and has actually just overcome that hurdle," I said.

"Are they on any medication?"

"Yes. Both babies were on caffeine. Now only William is on it. William is also on Ranitidine while Jessica was taken off it only yesterday," I said.

"Did you have fertility or do twins run in the family?" This question came as a blow to me. I didn't really want to go into the fertility side of things and walk down memory lane with a complete stranger.

"On my husband's side but two generations removed," I lied, but couldn't face the flood of questions I knew would follow. As I have scarcely spoken about the experience with my closest friends, it hardly seemed right to open up to this student. I knew that by omitting this information I was potentially affecting their research, but I didn't care to discuss my fertility issues.

As I answered the flood of questions, I could overhear Roxanne and thought how hard it must be for her as well. Roxanne had a two-year-old son, a toddler, and now had just had premature twins. What a nightmare!

"How were you during your pregnancy?" she continued.

"Fine, except for terribly sensitive skin. I had to be put onto cortisone cream. My blood pressure and everything else during pregnancy was normal," I said.

"So is it accurate to say then that there's no medical reason, except for the fact that your uterus was put under additional pressure with twins, for having them early?" she asked.

"I suppose that's accurate," I said, hoping this would be the last of the questions.

"One last question. How could you have better prepared for this experience?" What a question. I hadn't thought of it that way before.

"I don't think anything could ever prepare you for this," I said. "Is that all?" I had had enough of her questions. I felt exhausted.

"Yes. Thank you for your time." She got up and left the room.

I turned to Roxanne, a tear in my eyes and just smiled.

"Emma, are you alright?" she asked.

"Yep. Just a little rattled. I find it difficult reliving these past few weeks," I said.

"So do I. Nothing, absolutely nothing prepares you for what lies in store if your baby is born too soon. I had bought enough books; none covered this subject with enough insight. Until you've been here, you've no idea," Roxanne said.

"I often wonder what Jessica and William would have been like if they were born full term," I said.

"Don't go there Emma. You can't change anything now, you'll only feel like a failure." Roxanne seemed quite level headed about all of this. I blamed myself for their early arrival and could only pray there'd be no permanent scars.

Chapter Twelve

Mum arrived literally two days after my telephone call. Amazing! I was relieved to have another woman in the house, someone who could fully understand my emotional and somewhat paranoiac state. I had become like a lioness protecting her cubs and I think the hospital was beginning to regard me as a nuisance. I was at the hospital everyday from early morning until late evening and would either travel back with Benjamin or on my own if he wasn't going to be able to get there. I would have slept in the ward had there been room.

My babies on the other hand were loved by all the nurses and every one of them tried to get to look after Jessica and William at the start of each shift. I felt moved by their evident interest in the well being of my babies and I know that my presence and obvious concern for my children brought the nurses closer to them.

"Why don't you join me at the hospital after you've showered and changed," I said as I drove her home from the airport.

"I'd like to freshen up but I am dying to meet Jessica and William so I'll come as soon as I'm done." Mum was clearly nervous but excited at the same time.

I went on ahead to the hospital once I had dropped Mum at home and we had eaten a light breakfast together. Lillian was on duty that day.

As I walked through the security doors into the unit, I could sense an air of sadness. The nursing staff seemed a little less up beat and there was a discussion going on in the Intensive Care Unit amongst various members of staff. I called Lillian over to one side once I had settled my things down in the Special Care Unit.

"What's the matter today, everyone seems depressed?" I asked quietly, to avoid anyone overhearing my inquisitiveness.

"Yes, we lost a twenty-four week old baby in the early hours of the morning, Emma," Lillian said.

"Oh, how dreadful. What happened?" I asked knowing that I shouldn't pry.

"The baby's mother had pre-eclampsia and they had to deliver by emergency c-section. They baby's heart couldn't cope. The staff tried their very best but the baby was only four hundred and twenty grams and even his skin was barely formed," Lillian said.

As I listened to Lillian recount the tragic story I was grateful that I had managed to carry mine as far as I had, and no matter how traumatic I believed my circumstances to be, there was always someone experiencing a greater suffering. I was humbled.

"Emma, have your babies been bathed yet since they were born?" It seemed strange but they hadn't bathed during the first three weeks.

"Have the other mothers complained?" I asked jokingly.

"No, they're top and tailed twice a day so of course not. I think it would be good for them to experience a bath. Now that they're off the monitors I think it's time," Lillian said.

"Great, let's do it today. Their grandmother is coming in later and Benjamin will also be here so we can each bath a baby." Up until now Jessica and William had been too small and fragile to bath. It would have been too nerve-wracking to take them off the monitors to bath them in case they stopped breathing.

Two hours later my mother joined me in the unit.

"Mrs Hogan, there's a lady who says she's your mother at the door. Can we let her in?" the receptionist who operated the door to the unit asked.

"Yes. I had filled out the form to say she was coming today." What was the point of filling out the form in the first place if it wasn't to be read?

I went out to the passageway to meet her while she was hanging up her coat.

"Did you shower and freshen up?" I asked as we walked together toward the Special Care Unit.

"Yes, thanks. The roses smell gorgeous in the bathroom. So what are all these rooms for?"

"Let me show you the other units quickly. This is the Intensive Care Unit. All babies in here are in an incubator and most are younger than twenty-nine weeks but there are older babies who have medical problems in here also. Jessica was taken here after she stopped breathing." I walked Mum through the Intensive Care Unit; her face dropped as she peered into some of the incubators.

"Mum, don't stare, try to be discrete. It is upsetting for parents to see others peering into their babies' incubators especially if they're unwell," I suggested.

"Emma, they are tiny. How do they survive?" Mum was bewildered.

"Science and willpower," I said. "You'll be surprised what little fighters these premature babies are." Lillian called William 'The Fighter'.

"Here's the High Care Unit where William was to begin with." As I showed her the little ward the memories of my first visit with William came rushing back. I swallowed hard and quickly walked out of the room for some air.

"Are you alright darling?" she asked as she joined me in the passageway.

"Fine. I just feel claustrophobic at times in here."

As we walked towards the Special Care Unit she paused for a moment and hesitated.

"They're survivors," I urged, remembering how overwhelmed and giddy I felt at first in the unit.

"This is little Jessica," I said as I pointed to her crib where she lay asleep. "And this is little William. He's due for a feed," I said as William opened his eyes and began to yell.

"Would you like to pick him up?" Lillian joined us.

"Oh, Mum this is Lillian, the nurse I've been telling you about."

Her face had turned pale as she took in both Jessica and William.

"No, no. I'm a little nervous to hold them just now, give me a day or two," Mum said.

"How much sleep do they need a day?" she asked Lillian.

"Generally premature babies sleep a lot more during the day in the unit and wake at night. The noise and sheer number of people in the unit during the day is often too much for their little nervous systems to take and their brain to process, so their defence mechanism is to sleep and shut it out," Lillian said.

"They also weigh them at night."

"This can't be good for their routine once at home," Mum said.

"No, but we hope by that time they are bigger and stronger and they don't need to sleep so much during the day. It is, however, one of the challenges most parents of babies who've been in the unit have once their babies are at home. It's sometimes quite a difficult habit to break," Lillian said honestly.

"What are these for?" Mum pointed to the tube in their nostrils.

"That's how we feed them. Fortunately Jessica's almost exclusively breast-feeding now, just the night feeds we do via tube and William takes almost all his feeds by bottle now. We might take the tube away in the next few days and see how they do," Lillian said.

I picked William up and showed Mum the little dent in his heel where they had taken blood every second day for the first two weeks of his life. This would be one reminder for both of us of his days in the High Care Unit.

"We thought we'd bath them for the first time tonight," Lillian said.

"Haven't they been bathed since they were born?" Mum sounded surprised.

"No, they've been top and tailed twice daily. Too many tubes until now," I replied hastily.

"Oh, I'm sure they'll feel a whole lot better after a bath," Mum said, rather repulsed by the knowledge that her grandchildren hadn't been bathed for weeks.

She then watched as I fed William via tube and just as I finished his feed Jessica woke looking for hers. Lillian had tried to space their feeding times half an hour apart in order that she and I could cope better by feeding them in relays. Just as I laid William back in his crib a stream of milk ran from between his lips.

"What's wrong with William?"

"Oh, don't fret Mrs Sutherland," Lillian said, "it's only a little reflux. He's on two drugs for this right now to help with the burning sensation of the acid as well as the emptying of his stomach."

"William's addicted at the tender age of three weeks old!" I said jokingly but she looked distressed.

"I don't think it's serious," I went on as I tried to comfort her, but found it difficult as I myself hadn't the faintest idea what reflux really was, nor had I anticipated that it would affect William and us for that matter throughout the first year of his life.

As I lifted Jessica from her crib, negotiating the mass of tubing attached to her body parts, I turned to Mum and asked her if she wanted to hold Jessica before I put her onto my breast.

"I'm not sure I'm ready darling, she's also fragile," she hesitated.

"They're tougher than you think," I said, gesturing towards her to take Jessica from me.

"Perhaps if I sit here in your chair I'll be able to hold her on my lap in my arms." She started to warm to the idea.

All the while the baby boy in the corner of the room was crying incessantly, so Lillian had moved off to see to him, leaving us alone with Jessica.

This little boy came from a family of seven children, he being the eighth child. His siblings ranged in age from twenty-five to six years old. He was born full term but with a congenital lung and heart problem and had been in hospital for many weeks already.

His parents came from a simple background and his mother who had told me that she was forty-three, was devastated. She couldn't come to terms with the fact that she had given birth to seven healthy children so why was God punishing her with this last child.

One evening as I sat with Jessica and William while they slept, waiting for Benjamin to join me from work, she had told me a little about his story. She was sure the reason for his condition was because the nursing staff had left the window in the delivery room open while she was giving birth.

I suppose ordinarily I would have laughed at such ignorance or superstition, but having been dealt the cards I had with Jessica and William I, instead, felt deep, deep sympathy towards her. We all have our cross to bear.

I looked over at my mother who was quietly sitting with Jessica just gazing into her eyes and stroking her little arms.

"I think she's hungry Emma. Will you take her from me?" she said as I took Jessica into my arms and made myself comfortable.

"She's taking to the breast well," Mum remarked as she watched me feed.

"Yes, she's getting stronger everyday and suckles well now," I said.

"Emma, I've arranged for you to stay two nights in one of the overnight rooms this next week to help prepare you for home," Lillian said as she walked back over to where we were.

"How does this stay over actually work, Lillian?"

"Before we discharge any infant we make sure that at least one of the parents has stayed overnight and taken care of their baby in the room alone. We are on call, so should you need us during the night all you have to do is push the bell. It's important that you built up your confidence before you arrive home," Lillian said.

Hi Viv,

Jessica and William will be coming home soon. I'm excited after four long weeks in hospital. I can finally have my babies at home with me, but I'm also petrified. I've been spoilt in here with all the support. I'll have Mum for a while at home and Thembi of course, but I do feel a heavy burden and I haven't done any training to prepare for the race ahead. Am I guilty of being an ungrateful mother especially after the fertility treatment?

Actually, don't answer that question, I'd rather not know.

A student interviewed me and other mothers in the unit two days ago. It was like being put on a witness stand. The minute the babies were born, my days of privacy ended. It's great to have Mum here and to spend time with her, even if the only time we really spend together is either in hospital or late at night before going to bed. I think we're bonding like never before Viv, it's quite special you know. Dad's resorted to calling Mum 'my wishy-washy' because she's forever helping with the washing, ironing, cleaning while I'm at the hospital all day. I'm glad Dad isn't here, he'd have been bored stiff I think!

We're going to bath the babies today; do you remember the movie Cocoon? Well, it'll be something like that I imagine since they're bathed with towels on.

I'll let you know how this goes.

Love ya,
Emma-Beez

That evening we bathed Jessica and William. It was one of those quite extraordinary experiences, almost like a baptism. We wrapped Jessica and William in receiving blankets to keep them from losing too much body heat and to help make them feel secure. We then gently lowered them into their own bathtubs and slowly as the screaming subsided and they became acclimatised, we unfolded the blankets until they were lying fully naked, fully exposed in the bath water.

Jessica just loved the sensation of the water lapping against her body as Mum gently splashed water over her body. You could see by the sparkle in her sea blue eyes. William on the other hand felt uneasy and couldn't wait to be taken out and clothed.

Even from this early age, their characters were beginning to show themselves: William, always apprehensive of change while Jessica seemed to thrive on it.

I was due to stay overnight at the hospital for two nights, as Lillian had arranged, so the following day I packed my overnight bag, stuffed it with bra pads and travelled into the city with Mum.

"You sure you don't want me to join you?" Benjamin asked as Mum and I climbed into the car.

"Positive. I think you'll hate every minute of it, besides the beds are minute and you don't have breast milk!"

Had I have known I wouldn't have managed conveniently more than a half hour's sleep at any one stretch through the night, Benjamin could easily have slept in the bed, whilst I breast-fed Jessica, and bottle-fed William and expressed the entire night through! The nursing staff had neglected to inform me that the bed was a decoy.

Mum left the hospital at around six thirty, by which time she was exhausted having driven in with me earlier that morning. She was going home to cook supper for Benjamin and herself.

I felt isolated and alone. I was overwhelmed by the thought of my responsibilities, which without the safety net of the hospital staff, were only beginning. How was I going to cope once she returned to South Africa? I knew I had Thembi Mbena, a maternity nurse from South Africa, but that didn't seem the same as having my own mother around.

I decided not to have Jessica and William with me in the room; I felt it was just too much to ask of me on my own. The staff at the hospital agreed so I was to be called each time either Jessica or William woke for a feed.

What a nightmare! Jessica woke every two and a half hours looking for milk while William woke every three. I might as well have climbed into Jessica's crib naked and let her suckle whenever she chose to.

"Patricia, can we agree that you'll feed William while I feed Jessica, it's just too much for me?" I pleaded with Patricia, the night sister, at about one thirty the following morning.

"Sure, will you have help at home?" She obviously wanted to know how I'd cope at home if I were on my own and Benjamin had to get a good night's sleep for work the following day.

"Yes, I've got a maternity nurse coming in from South Africa day after tomorrow," I said, rather relieved that I had planned this in advance. "I'll bring her in to meet everyone. I've already made plans for her to meet Lillian so that she can get some advice on how to make the transition home as easy as possible."

"Fine, then she'll be able to help you through the night," Patricia said.

"How are you feeling?" Benjamin called early the following morning.

"Terrible. Like death warmed up. I think I might have had three hours of broken sleep. My boobs hurt, they're full of milk and so hard you could crack an egg against them!" I said.

"Why don't you forget about tonight and come home?" Benjamin urged.

"I can't. It's one more night and if it goes smoothly, the babies can come home in the next few days."

"Can't you see that breast expert about your boobs?" Benjamin asked.

"The one without children, sure but what can she really do to help me?" I asked irritably.

"That's where her expertise lies, she must have some advice for engorged breasts," Benjamin said.

"I think I'll wait for Mum to come in, she'll know what to do. She's breast-fed three kids," I said.

"Fine, you're boss." Benjamin backed down. "It doesn't matter what I say Emma, I'm always wrong aren't I?" Benjamin said.

"What do you mean?" I asked defensively.

"I'm trying my best Emma to be supportive, but nothing I say is ever right and you're always on the defensive." Benjamin had obviously been living with this pent-up frustration for weeks and I'd been completely oblivious to the fact, so caught up in my own world.

When my mother arrived later that morning I asked her what she would recommend.

"Oh, you must be in pain," she said as she hugged me.

"I'm in agony and have so much milk I'm not sure what to do with it."

"Here's what I recommend you do. I'll buy some cabbages and put them in the fridge for you so that when you get home tomorrow evening they'll be ready. In the meantime massage your breast while you express and try to cut back on your expressing for William. That together with breast-feeding Jessica is causing havoc with your boobs. They're being over stimulated."

"How often should I express then?" I asked, as I had been expressing four hourly and feeding Jessica in between. Despite this I still had tons of milk.

"I'd express first thing in the morning and then at midday and again last thing before you go to bed at night," Mum advised.

"That's half the amount I'm doing now," I exclaimed.

"Yes, but do this gradually, cutting out one express time every three days," Mum said.

"But what happens when William demands more milk and he's not suckling to stimulate the increase," I asked, totally confused as to how I was ever going to cater for both William and Jessica's increasing demand for milk when Jessica was the only one suckling to help stimulate my milk flow. In my humble opinion, the only way I was going to cater for William's demands was to express regularly.

"What are the cabbage leaves for?" I asked inquiringly.

"Oh, they're great for engorged breast, they help to reduce the swelling and calm the milk flow, something in the leaves themselves."

"Emma, I would use cool flannels on your breasts after each breast feed in the meantime," Mum said.

I grinned as I saw myself walking through the shopping malls with cabbage leaves in my brassiere. I would redefine the padded bra with my own unique fashion statement!

Dear Viv,

I think I'm a cow in more than one sense of the word!
Not only am I full of milk but according to Benjamin I'm also full of sh...t! I can't help being so short fused right now

and intolerant. It's frightening, sometimes I don't even recognise myself. I'm hoping it will pass and this is just a phase, if not I think I'll be looking for another husband!

We took the babies home today from the hospital. It was raining buckets this morning when we arrived at the hospital and of course there was nowhere to park. I still can't understand how you can have a hospital with very sick people coming and going and not provide parking. That's why Benjamin and hundreds of husbands like him get traffic fines when they take their wives into hospital to give birth. You should have seen us in the car, packed to the hilt. Mum upfront with Benjamin, myself jammed between the two car seats like a ham sandwich and Thembi squeezed in the boot at the back between the back seat and rear window. No one wanted to miss out on the action. Mum's been great. Although she has stepped on Benjamin's toes a little, especially when they're alone in the same room together. I suppose it's just the in-law syndrome. The ward staff all gathered around to say their goodbyes, it was quite moving. We were reminded what to do if they stopped breathing and started choking, something I hope never happens. It's easy resuscitating a doll, it's another thing an actual child and yours at that! I haven't told the hospital because they said I shouldn't on any account, but I hired two apnoea mats anyway.

I'll be up at night to feed I'm sure, so I don't want to have to stay up the whole night listening to their breathing to make sure they're still alive.

You would have laughed to see Benjamin carrying them out in their car seats. You could barely see them, dwarfed by the seats themselves. They don't make car seats small enough!

They're safe at home now and thank goodness Mum's still here. I'm petrified!

I don't know what I had imagined motherhood would be like Viv, but honestly it wasn't remotely like this that's for sure.

Thembi had met with Lillian who had advised her to recreate as similar an environment for the first week at home as possible to that back in the hospital. That way we'd help reduce any trauma. Hence why Thembi had urged me to put the babies in one cot, lying lengthways side-by-side swaddled in receiving blankets. Over the cot Thembi had placed a sheet to make the space above their heads seem less daunting. I must say it all looked quite ridiculous but served a purpose I suppose.

Jessica woke at least six times during the night and screamed blue murder right into William's ear. This she did on a regular basis. We decided to swap their positions in the cot everyday to help prevent William's ears from bursting. My mother nicknamed Jessica the 'wild banshee'.

"What can it be?" I asked Benjamin one night as we lay awake in our bed waiting for Jessica to begin her nightly ritual.

"It's colic I think," Benjamin suggested yawning.

Thembi usually bottle-fed the babies during the night, as they were feeding every three hours. Although I knew Thembi was there and that's what we were paying her for, I would still wake each time either Jessica or William cried, I could not help myself.

"Can't you find some anti-colic medication?"

"Yes, but I've tried them all, there's nothing on the market that seems to help. I'm beginning to think that colic is a lazy term used for everything and anything that keeps tiny babies up at night yelling. It could be anything for all I know," I said fed up.

"I know you're exhausted but try to stay calm, all babies cry and everyone says the first three months are hell," Benjamin tried to console me.

Sure, fine, you get to go to work everyday, while I'm the one having to cope with both babies' idiosyncrasies all day. I'm not sure what's easier, I thought to myself.

Mum eventually recommended something from South Africa, not available on the UK market.

"Why don't you try 'Bennett's' colic mixture, everyone I've spoken to in South Africa says it works magic."

"What's the formula and why can't you get it here if it's so effective?" I asked suspiciously.

"I'm not sure, but it's worth a try, nothing else seems to be working. I can get Fiona to bring it with her next week, she's coming to London for a few days on her way to Europe," Mum suggested.

"What the heck! I'm not having much joy with anything else," I gave in.

Little did I know that it wasn't colic after all!

It was gastro-oesophageal reflux – a condition, which Jessica would outgrow in the months to come, unlike her brother, whose condition was to become progressively worse.

The Health Visitor kindly offered to visit me at home each week especially for the first few months until the babies were a little older and I had mastered the art of getting around with two babies.

It was certainly an art, as I soon discovered when Thembi and I tried to get our double buggy into any shopping mall and around the hundreds of display racks. It was almost impossible and nine times out of ten I decided not to take them with me, it was just too much hassle and I imagined would eventually cost me buckets as I knocked over carefully constructed displays.

"Emma, how are things going this week?" Sue the Health Visitor asked one Tuesday morning during her regular scheduled visit.

"Not so well, both babies are such difficult eaters especially William. He simply arches his back, turns his head away as if in extreme pain and cries. Thembi and I spend hours trying to get enough milk into him each feed, there's no time for anything else," I said quite exhausted, three weeks having passed since the babies had been discharged from St Mary's Hospital. Sue had asked the same question every week and I had given her the same answer. I wondered if I was not communicating well enough because she seemed not to be concerned and certainly had no insightful suggestions for me as how to cope with or address the problem.

"Let's see how much they weigh," Sue suggested as I undressed Jessica while Thembi held William.

Jessica hated lying on her back and every time I laid her onto the changing unit to get undressed or dressed before or after a bath, she would scream her lungs out, kicking her arms and legs in the air. All this commotion made it a whole lot harder and as a result the procedure took far longer than it should have done aggravating the situation even further.

As Sue placed Jessica on the scales I turned and looked away, it had become my worst nightmare these weighing sessions. I almost felt like I was taking an exam only I had no control over the outcome and no matter how hard I had studied I would fail every time.

This week Jessica had put on a surprisingly large amount of weight relatively speaking, two hundred and twenty grams, wow! I looked over at Thembi and smiled.

Thembi seemed pleased that her efforts had this week resulted in significant weight gain unlike most other weeks, when both babies just weren't gaining enough.

"How is Jessica generally?" Sue asked, as Thembi put her clothes back on again and took her through to the TV room to give her a bottle of expressed breast milk.

"As I said before, feeding is problematic, although not as difficult as with William. She also wakes up at night screaming like a 'banshee'," I said.

"Have you tried a different teat?"

Have I tried a different teat? I thought to myself. If only Sue knew the lengths I had gone to, to find every teat available on the UK market. In desperation I had called the teat manufacturers themselves and written down lists of all the teats they had produced and where I could purchase them, including all teats for premature babies, the ones they used in the neonatal wards. Some I had had to buy in lots of a hundred since most manufacturers only sold them in bulk and mostly to retailers and hospitals, so I had a cupboard full of unused teats as Thembi and I worked our way through every one of them. What was even more soul destroying was the fact that William and Jessica didn't like the same teat. Eventually I settled for a Nuk teat for William and an Avent teat for Jessica. One was wide necked and the other narrow, which meant I also had to invest in different bottles. Well you can imagine, I became the teat and bottle expert overnight!

"Sue, I've tried that. I've also tried different feeding positions. Some days William will only feed if he faces forwards with his head cocked to the side above my shoulder," I said, to stop Sue from going down that path, as although I didn't know what the problem was, I certainly knew that it wasn't the teat, or the bottle or the position, it was something far greater.

I undressed William who by this time was screaming from hunger. I was late with his feed. That wasn't difficult as Jessica and he were feeding every three hours and that was three hours from the start of one feed to the start of another and bearing in mind it took us over and hour to feed them, they were in effect feeding every two hours! Sue weighed William and again to my surprise he had gained slightly more than Jessica.

"Well, even though you've been struggling to feed them, they've put on good weight this week."

"Yes, but William appears to be in some sort of pain when he feeds. He arches his back, turns his head away and often refuses to feed, crying incessantly," I said, trying to get Sue to take notice and recommend a course of action.

"I'm sure it is just colic and it will sort itself out," Sue said.

"Do you think he could have a milk allergy or be lactose intolerant?" I asked knowing Phoebe's daughter had been and

I had heard of numerous other babies who had been diagnosed only too late.

"No, he wouldn't be allergic to breast milk." Sue was adamant.

"But there's lactose in breast milk," I protested.

"Emma, I'm sure it will sort itself out soon enough. Have you tried putting him on the breast again?" Sue continued ignoring my protests.

"Yes, I've tried thinking he would be more willing now he's bigger but he just screams when I try to get him to latch," I said.

"Keep trying now and again," Sue suggested.

"I've told him he's missing out and one day he'll have to start liking breasts, he's a boy after all." I tried to sound chipper about the situation but deep down was becoming desperate.

The situation continued and, contrary to Sue and the GP's advice, things didn't get better. In fact William began to vomit as the volume of milk at feed times was increased.

I had this gut feeling that something was horribly wrong and that William's prematurity had left a scar.

I was damned if I was going to sit back and endure this, I was determined to find out what was wrong.

Chapter Thirteen

Dear Viv,

We've been home for four weeks now and things only seem to be getting harder. Mum returned to South Africa last week, I cried for two hours solid.

I was always told feeding babies was easy: just stick a bottle in their mouth. Well, so much for friendly advice.

From the minute we arrived home feeding has been a complete nightmare, a nightmare of such magnitude you couldn't imagine Viv, not even in your wildest dreams. Not even Dr Spock could have experienced this. It takes Thembi and I an hour and a half at a time to feed each baby and even then they're not taking what the Health Visitor says they should be taking in volume. There's not an ounce of fat on their tiny bones.

I can't understand why some medical guru hasn't invented an alternative to breast or formula milk yet.

You remember the friend I used to play hockey with, Phoebe Carlyle, well she's my pillar of strength. She recommended I buy a book called 'The Contented Baby Book' by Gina Ford. It's like a bible for many mothers around here and they swear by it. All I can say after reading it cover to cover and then a second time, it only confirms my convictions that Jessica and William have come from planet Mars.

They defy every aspect of the book from the quantity of milk they should be taking, to their birth weights, to their sleeping patterns. None of her schedules work for me because when it should only take a half hour for the baby to drink its bottle, it takes mine an hour and a half. I'm always lagging a feed and a sleep behind the schedule! And as far as sleeping goes, well they don't.

It doesn't matter how many times I've tried this so called 'controlled crying method' where you are supposed to let your baby cry itself to sleep out of pure exhaustion, mine just land up vomiting all the milk Thembi and I have just spent the last hour and a half struggling to get into them. We then have to start the whole process over again before they'll even think about going back to sleep.

On leaving the hospital I was instructed to give Jessica and William a dose of iron, vitamins and folic acid on a daily basis until they're a year old. Being as conscientious a mother as I am, I've followed their instructions to the letter, but sadly Jessica has decided to copy her brother. She thinks I'm giving him too much attention so she has decided to start vomiting. Instead of regularly vomiting her milk, she's intent on vomiting the iron I give her. It's almost instantaneous – as soon as it hits her stomach it comes straight back up. So, I've canned the iron knowing full well it's the one thing they really need being prem.

You should see our newly laid wool sisal carpets: they're slowly turning a paler shade of white. We're now feeding William in the bathroom to try and prevent any more mishaps on the carpets, but the view isn't particularly interesting.

If you know of a good carpet cleaning method, I've tried the water, sponge and hair dryer method already, just let me know.

Love you
Emma-Beez

"Benjamin," I said as he stepped out of the shower.
"Yes."

"William's vomiting is not normal, I'm worried. What should I do?"

"Why don't you find a private paediatrician and see if they can advise you? Maybe they are allergic to milk and have a lactose intolerance and that's why William pulls away arching his back all the time or worse, vomits it back up, and why Jessica fights her feeds." Benjamin had a great idea. Up until now I hadn't thought about a private paediatrician since the NHS system seemed to be the only option. Unlike in South Africa where I would have been assigned a paediatrician immediately in hospital before being discharged after the birth.

"I'll look into it. I'm not sure how I even go about trying to find one in Surrey who's close by, but I'll ask around."

"I'll ask a few people at work and see what they do," Benjamin suggested.

"I don't trust the diagnostic capabilities of most of the GPs here," I said honestly.

As the weeks passed by and feeding became more and more of an ordeal with very little time for anything else, so I grew increasingly frustrated. I began to feel trapped within the confines of our home. Where other new mothers found solace in meeting with their NCT group or with friends, I couldn't for fear of William vomiting all over someone's sofa or out of embarrassment at his yelling while I forced him to take some milk. Anyone looking at me would have called the child abuse line accusing me of force-feeding my child and making him eat against his will. Well, it was the only way I could get him to take anything; he would have died if Thembi and I hadn't dedicated our time to making sure he was getting enough to eat. Left to his own devices William would have starved, the pain of the burning acid was just so great for him.

I had heard about postnatal depression, but I hadn't time to think long enough about my situation to get depressed, that would come later and it most certainly did.

During the first four months I had spoken to work a few times and contacted Jenny Green to keep up to date with what was happening at work. To be honest it was a pleasant distraction for a half hour or so and reminded me of what my life without children had been like.

"Hi Emma." Jenny sounded surprised to hear my voice.

"I thought I'd call in and see how you were getting along."

"Oh, I've been away in New York and Washington for a few days working on the marketing roll-out strategy for one of the new solutions."

"How are we doing with those we rolled out just after I went on maternity leave?" I asked curious to know if we had started to make money out of those solutions yet.

"Slow, but we've just landed a large four year contract with Bell in the US," she said.

"How are things going with Allan Crawford?" I asked. Allan had taken over from Mark after he had resigned, at the same time as the start of my maternity leave. I had never worked with him before and wondered how Jenny was handling things.

"Fine, he actually offered me a job last week while we were in the US together." As Jenny said this I thought how strange this was. Allan offering a contractor a job when he knew full well I was returning to work in the September, after six months' maternity leave. I decided not to say anything.

"Oh, I suppose you would then be working with me once I return," I said as casually as I could.

"Well, Emma, do you really want to come back? You've got a great home, a fantastic husband and now two adorable children. Why would you want to come back to work, it's chaos here as always?"

Something fishy was going on, did Jenny have a hidden agenda and did she have one from the day she stepped into my shoes? If so, she had obviously done this sort of thing before. I'd give Allan a call myself in the next day or so.

Having done my homework, I eventually found a private hospital in Surrey and there I discovered two paediatricians.

I didn't have the faintest idea which of the two to choose, so randomly picked one, Dr Marlow.

As it turned out he was one of the most handsome doctors I'd met in the UK, which when you've had it so difficult is a pleasant distraction and at least makes the appointments more interesting! I had made an appointment and felt relieved when his secretary said how busy he was. Busy had always meant good to me, but assumptions are just that, assumptions not reality.

"Hi Mrs Hogan, please do come in," Dr Marlow said as he greeted Thembi and me.

"This is my maternity nurse, Thembi and this is Jessica and this is William," I said as we all sat down, Jessica on my lap and William on Thembi's.

"What can I do for you today?" Dr Marlow asked.

"I'd like to agree to you being my paediatrician for Jessica and William. Being premature babies I'd feel more comfortable having a paediatrician than relying exclusively on the NHS system."

"That's fine, most of my patients' parents feel the same way," Dr Marlow said. "Tell me a little about Jessica and then a little about William, do you have their red books with you?"

As I handed him the little books I was given by the hospital before discharge, my heart felt heavy as I thought of what we as a family had been through these past four and a half months and how difficult Jessica and William's short lives had been thus far.

I recounted their history and told Dr Marlow about their birth, their hospital stay, their feeding problems and their sleeping problems, paying particular attention to William.

"It sounds to me as if William might have what we call reflux. Let's examine them, weigh them and take their lengths and then I'll tell you a little more about reflux and what to expect," Dr Marlow said.

"Jessica has a little strawberry mark, this will more than likely fade and drop off in time, no need to worry about it," Dr Marlow said as he weighed Jessica, took her length and head circumference and examined her hips, stomach, glands and other bodily parts.

He did the same for William and found nothing out of the ordinary.

"Now, reflux is the term used for the condition where people bring back acid fluid from the stomach after eating or drinking. This is due to an under developed sphincter. In adults the condition is often referred to as heart burn or indigestion," Dr Marlow said.

"William had reflux in hospital, but they said it wasn't serious. How do you treat reflux?"

"I will prescribe an anti-acid medication and I would recommend you thicken William's milk feeds," Dr Marlow said.

"Should I put him on formula milk?" I asked, wanting him to say yes which would let me off the hook.

"No. You can still give him breast milk but just add two scoops of thickening agent to it," he said. "I would also feed him as upright as possible and keep him upright for at least a half hour after each feed."

"I've tried every feeding position there is, none help. In fact he prefers to feed lying in my arms with his head cocked backwards to the side," I said, thinking how peculiar all this was.

"Well then, feed him in whichever position works," Dr Marlow said.

I wasn't sure whether this appointment made me feel relieved or disappointed. I had confirmation about William's reflux and had some medication now to give him, but I had an uneasy feeling that this wasn't the answer, or at least the one that would put an end to this nightmare.

"Benjamin, you never seem to talk to me anymore. I don't know what you are feeling and you never share your thoughts with me, what's the matter?" I asked at nine o'clock one evening as we ate dinner, the babies having just been put to bed.

"Nothing's wrong," Benjamin said and continued to eat his dinner in silence.

"Yes, there is." I removed his plate from under him and stared him in the eyes.

"Do you really want to have this conversation now, I'm tired," Benjamin said.

"Yes. Are you having an affair?" I asked just like that.

He looked at me and turning away he said:

"I wish I were sometimes Emma, but when do you think I have the time to cheat? I'm either at work or doing babies twenty-four hours a day it seems," Benjamin replied.

"What do you mean by I wish I were?" Now, acutely aware that Benjamin must be deeply unhappy for him to say something like this.

"Well, you don't want to hear this Emma, but you're an emotional wreck and you're always irritable and on the defensive, nothing I say is right," Benjamin said as he pulled his plate back towards him to finish his meal.

"Well, I'm sure you'd also behave like this if you lived on three hours of broken sleep a night and had to look after these babies twenty-four hours a day with no other distractions." As I said this I realised I had taken the defensive role as if Benjamin were accusing me of something.

"I'm sorry," I said backing down.

"You see what I mean Emma?"

"I just can't stand it Benjamin. I ask everyday if this nightmare will end and I'll wake up. William is suffering and no one seems to be able to help. Why have we been dealt such a rough time? It's not supposed to be like this," I asked, knowing there wasn't an answer.

"How can I possibly be having an affair Emma? You are so naïve. I love you more than my own life, you and the babies mean the world to me. I'm just completely exhausted. I have to sleep on the train into the City every morning because I'm so knackered and I have developed this rash which won't seem to go away," he said, opening up finally.

"What rash? Show me."

"No, just leave me Emma." Benjamin sounded irritated.

"Let me see, you need to see someone about it," I said, as he finally showed me the rash, which ran down his chest, to his stomach and to the inner part of his thighs.

Taken aback at how unobservant I had been and realising how little attention I had been giving Benjamin, I burst into tears.

"I'm so sorry. I'm so ill prepared that's all, I'm not coping very well," I said.

As it turned out Benjamin had a fungal infection brought about by high levels of stress.

Darling Viv,

I confronted Benjamin today about possibly having an affair. I feel rather stupid now, but at the time it did seem as if he might be Viv. He's so distant, a stranger in our own home.

He has compelling reasons to be this way, especially seeing his wife is a wreck, a hag and a short tempered cow. To make things worse I'm feeling so unattractive, I'm often still in my nightdress at noon!

All we talk about when we're alone together are the babies, which after the days I'm having is the last thing I'd like to discuss. I don't know when we last slept through the night. We have started lying in bed listening for them to wake and then waiting for Thembi to finish feeding them. I think you'd call us paranoid and perhaps we are. I've turned to taking my frustrations out on Benjamin and often phone him in the middle of his working day in tears, telling him that I can't do this anymore and that if I have to clean up one more vomit or one more dirty nappy I'll throw up myself.

The more emotionally unstable I become, the more distant Benjamin becomes.

I've been seeing a private paediatrician and even he hasn't helped William's reflux.

Enough self-pity!

I'm still breast-feeding and yes, hating every minute of it. My boobs are like balloons and the buttons on my blouses won't stay shut. If I'm not being suctioned by Jessica then I'm being suctioned by the breast pump every four hours, it's such fun!

Just such fun!

I've assembled quite a collection of breast pumps, three to be precise. One's a supersonic dual breast pump, like the hospitals use and the other two identical ones are a little gentler on my nipples. I have two just in case one gives up on me through over usage. I think I might give up soon, it's almost six months and my milk is beginning to resemble sugared water. William's refusing it more and more and I think he associates it with the pain in his oesophagus caused by reflux. And Jessica prefers the bottle now; she only really takes from my boob last thing at night as a comfort drink.

I sometimes think you were wise not to marry and not to have children.

Lots of love
Emma-Beez

I had thought about work often since my telephone conversation with Jenny and decided to call Allan Crawford to find out what was going on and to discuss my role going forward.

"Hi Allan. How are you?"

"Hi Emma, good to hear from you. How are the twins?"

"Well thanks," I lied, but didn't want work to know what difficult a time I had for fear they'd be loath to bring me back on board in a senior position, thinking I'd be distracted. Allan's wife had also just had a second child, a little girl and he was forever bragging about how well she was thriving, which just made me feel all the more inadequate with mine.

"I've been meaning to call you for a few days, but I've been travelling on and off the past few weeks and the time zones have clashed." I knew he was exaggerating for effect.

"I thought I'd contact you seeing I'm going to be back within the next two months as agreed. We need to discuss what role you think I can fill seeing the structure has changed again." I had heard via colleagues how the structure had changed yet again and how another round of retrenchments had been undertaken.

"Yes, I'm working on that now. What do you want to do Emma?" Allan asked, as an easy way to avoid answering me directly.

"Allan, I'm keen to pursue the marketing required for strategic alliances as well as develop our customer relations side. I would need more flexible working hours as you know, so we'd need to work something out." I had already, early on, warned them I'd want flexible working hours at least for the first few months back until I was comfortable that the babies had settled well with our new nanny, Thembi having returned to South Africa.

"Well sounds good, let me work on a job description plus remuneration structure and get this to you next week. I'll then give you a call and we can go from there."

"You have my e-mail, send it to that address, I'll expect something next week then," I said, confirming the timing.

"Please send my regards to Benjamin. Cheers," Allan said as he hung up. I got the feeling that he was buying time and he hadn't done anything in preparation for my return to work. I needed to see Jenny Green's contract to see if the terms and conditions I had negotiated with her, had changed in the interim. I'd have to call my colleague in legal.

Dr Marlow had said with confidence that William's reflux would improve as he began to sit upright, to crawl and eventually to walk. He also said it would improve with the introduction of solids as these were heavier and harder to bring back than milk. William and Jessica were now approaching six months and still his reflux persisted, in fact it had got worse.

Sally-Ann, our new nanny, brought a change of clothes with her everyday just in case and sure enough she'd need them.

"Emma, you know I've lost two stone in weight since I joined you. It must be walking round the house feeding William," Sally-Ann said one morning.

Sally-Ann had struck a chord with William and fortunately for me, he now fed mostly with her during the day, and Benjamin and I took it in turns at night to feed him, depending on who didn't mind getting wet and having to change!

Although Jessica's feeding had improved, it had taken Sally-Ann and I two weeks to get her onto a formula she'd take. I even resorted to buying a small container of every available formula on the market and preparing a glass of each for Benjamin to taste to see which he'd prefer, assuming his taste buds were similar to Jessica's.

"Emma, these are disgusting!" Benjamin exclaimed, as he tasted them. "They taste like sawdust."

"Just think of it as if you were at a wine tasting in Stellenbosch," I said, trying to get his mind off what it was he was drinking.

"That's pretty hard to do. I don't have that good an imagination," he said as he sipped the last cup of formula milk.

"Well, what's your verdict?" I asked, waiting impatiently.

"Before I tell you, answer one question for me."

"Sure," I said.

"Why is it that I had to taste the milks and not you?" he asked smiling.

"I've already tasted them," I lied.

"Yes, sure Emma. I believe you."

"I think I'd go for the Cow and Gate or the Aptamil, the rest suck," he said as he went to the bathroom to wash his mouth out with water.

Sally-Ann and I would arrive each month at Dr Marlow's rooms with the same sob story about William's eating but alas we were sent away with the same unsatisfactory reply every time.

"William will grow out of it. I know it's hard but I have babies a whole lot worse than William," Dr Marlow would repeatedly say.

I'm convinced he thought I was just another neurotic mother and that I exaggerated the severity of the situation. Had he only visited my house to see the carpet stains, he would have known that I wasn't.

I felt at a loss for what to do, not being a native I wasn't familiar with the medical profession and I certainly didn't have the network of contacts here that I would ordinarily have drawn upon.

My only alternative and perhaps my saving grace was that Benjamin, the twins and I were all travelling to South Africa for Christmas. I could seek professional advice once I was back there. That was only eleven long weeks away!

Chapter Fourteen

Two weeks later Benjamin and I found ourselves at the hospital with William. He had literally stopped eating. No matter how hard I tried he wouldn't drink his milk and neither would he eat his fruit, vegetables or cereal. (That was all he was on in terms of solids at this point.) In desperation I called Benjamin at work.

"William's not eating darling, he simply refuses by turning his head away. He hasn't eaten since yesterday and only takes a few sips of milk at a time, I'm getting worried," I said, tears streaming down my cheeks.

"Is it any different to how he usually is?" Benjamin asked, used to my frantic calls during the middle of his workday.

"Darn it Benjamin, I'm serious, he's going to dehydrate first and then die of starvation if we don't get him to the hospital!" I yelled down the receiver.

"Emma, calm down to a panic. I'll get on the next train home, wait for me," Benjamin said, realising how serious the situation obviously had become.

Sally-Ann and I waited for Benjamin and in the meantime we kept trying to get William to take some milk. He simply refused. I could see his face growing paler and paler and black rings starting to form under his eyes.

I couldn't take it any longer, so called Benjamin on his mobile phone.

"Emma, I'm hurrying as fast as I can. I'm about fifteen minutes from Woking train station," Benjamin said even before I could say a word.

"It's bad Benjamin. I'll fetch you from the station. Meet me outside and we can go to the Royal Surrey Hospital from there."

"What about Jessica?" I hadn't thought about her and suddenly I felt really guilty. William had demanded so much of my time since his birth that Jessica, who was naturally more independent, had had to get on with things.

I turned to Sally-Ann and asked her if she would baby-sit that night until we returned with or without William from the hospital.

"Sally-Ann says she'll stay as long as need be until we come home tonight. She'll put Jessica to bed."

"Good. Just wait for me at the north side of the station exit."

I sat at the station for ten minutes waiting for Benjamin to arrive and when he did I barely gave him time to get into the car.

"Emma, this is the time when you need to be calmer than ever. Slow down, William needs you to be level headed," he instructed, as he sat down in the back of the car next to William and stroked his head.

"I'm trying, it's not easy."

My mother always told me that opposites attract and that often a cool headed, calm individual married a free-spirited, fiery one. That summed us up quite accurately.

We arrived at the hospital, parked the car and made our way towards the Accident and Emergencies section of the hospital.

I had called Dr Marlow in the meantime and he was there to greet us. Something both Benjamin and I were quite impressed about when we look back on the sequence of events.

"Hello, you must be Mr Hogan, pleased to meet you," Dr Marlow said as he came up to the reception desk where we stood.

"Mrs Hogan, so what's the story with William."

"The usual, except this time he really isn't eating, he stopped eating solids about twenty-four hours ago and he will only sip his milk."

"Now look here young fellow, you've got to eat to grow and stay strong. Why have you been giving your parents such a hard time?" he said, as he lent over and spoke directly to William as if he could understand. I was moved by his gentleness with William.

"Look, I wore your favourite tie William, the one with the 'airplanes'." Benjamin had taken a liking to Dr Marlow's tie with aeroplanes on it the last time we saw him.

Dr Marlow led us into a side room where he asked if I had a bottle of milk with me. I handed him William's formula bottle and he tried to get William to feed. William threw his head from side to side and turned away immediately. No amount of coaxing would get him to drink his milk.

"Mrs Hogan I don't believe there's anything wrong except his reflux as I've told you before," Dr Marlow said.

"Well, if that's the case the medication isn't working and neither is the food thickener. He is still vomiting copious amounts and still arching his back and refusing to feed," I said a little irritated.

"Dr Marlow, we would appreciate it if you would run a few tests to be sure there isn't anything else wrong with William," Benjamin interjected.

"I will do so, but I'm sure we'll find nothing out of the ordinary," Dr Marlow said with conviction.

I was about to protest when Benjamin stamped my foot.

"Thank you," he said.

"We'll test for any allergies and lactose intolerance for which we'll need a stool sample. I'll check for any kidney abnormalities as you specifically requested Mrs Hogan and I'll admit him and we'll monitor him for a while," Dr Marlow said and then added, "He's not dehydrated and he seems chirpy to me."

"Yes I know that's our William – he always looks at the bright side of life."

As Dr Marlow left the room and called a nurse over giving her instructions, I turned to Benjamin.

"What were you thinking back there, my foot hurts?"

"You can't afford to piss him off Emma, won't get very far with that approach. Let's see what the tests bring back and go from there."

"Why can't he take a look down William's throat, after all that's where the problem is isn't it?" Stating what I thought was the obvious thing to do.

"Emma, I'm not the enemy here. You're behaving like a madwoman. I don't have the answer but my best guess would be that it's invasive surgery you're suggesting and he's not a paediatric surgeon. I suppose he isn't ready to go to those lengths yet," Benjamin said, but he knew I wasn't happy with his answer.

"How am I ever going to get William's stool, he hasn't eaten anything!" We followed the nurse to the neonatal ward.

"We'll just have to persevere with his milk until he does take enough," Benjamin said.

"Well, you try. I've tried for the last twelve hours and failed," I said fed up.

Benjamin took William in his arms and sat down in the corner with a chair. Slowly but slowly William began to take a little milk. Only a few millilitres at first and then more.

"Maybe I should go to work and you should stay at home!"

We spent the rest of the day and well into the evening at the hospital. As Dr Marlow had suspected the tests he did all came back negative.

"I'm afraid it's as I suspected."

As we drove William home late that night, my heart felt heavy and I knew we were letting William down, he was clearly suffering and as hard as I tried nobody seemed to listen.

I decided to contact Anthony in the legal department. He had worked with me on drafting Jenny Green's original contract. I thought I would approach him and see if I could wrangle a copy.

"Anthony, how are you?"

"Wow, Emma, long time no hear. I'm fine, how are the twins?"

"They're growing up each day. A handful though," I said, not wanting to go into any more detail than this.

"I've got three and I can't imagine what two at one time must be like. Why the call Emma?"

"I need to ask a favour of you."

"Sure, shoot," Anthony said, not at all hesitant.

"You know the contract we worked on together for the contractor I brought on board while I was on maternity leave?" I asked.

"Mmm yes, Jenny Green I think her name was."

"That's her. I seem to have misplaced my copy of the final contract, could you forward one to me?" I asked.

"Well, which one are you looking for?"

Now aware there was more than one, I began to believe that my suspicions were probably correct about what was going on behind the scenes.

"The one that's current," I said, trying to sound as if I knew there was more than one in the first instance.

"Sure, what's your e-mail address?"

I gave Anthony my e-mail address and then suddenly thought it would be better if I could compare the terms of the original with those of the current one.

"On second thoughts, Anthony, won't you forward the current as well as the original contract?"

"Consider it done. When are you coming back?"

"My intentions are beginning of September," I said.

"We miss you around the office," Anthony said as we said goodbye and replaced our receivers.

The next call I made was to Jenny Green.

"Hi Emma, I'm surprised to hear your voice. How are you?"

"I'm well thanks. Just called to check in."

Jenny gave me a run down of the very basics and then went on to tell me how chaotic the office was and how I just wouldn't like coming back.

"Thanks Jenny you've already mentioned this to me during our last conversation. I still intend to come back in September as originally planned."

With that there was a deathly silence on the other end of the telephone.

"Jenny, I need to see a copy of the current contract please that you and Allan Crawford drew up together," I said with authority.

"Oh, why Emma?"

"I need to understand if there is an overlap period when I return, so that there's time for a handover period back to me," I said, trying to think of a legitimate excuse which wouldn't raise alarm bells for her.

"Let me talk to Allan first and I'll get back to you."

She's definitely hiding something I thought to myself; at least I'll have a copy from legal. Until I knew what was going on I would wait to call Allan.

Hi Viv,

A quick note to let you know that I think William's eating is improving, Jessica's certainly on the up and up. William only vomits once a day at worst now, so I'm saving on washing powder and ironing. Jessica's crawling and now into everything she can lay her hands on. She seems to be delighted and amazed at her own accomplishments. William's not what I would say crawling, he is doing some kind of leopard crawl on his stomach; perhaps his muscles aren't strong enough yet or he's been watching too much television. I've found a paediatrician, Dr Marlow, and have been going to him now for over eight weeks. You'd melt he's so good looking. He says William's reflux will go in time as he outgrows it. I do hope so, but I'm afraid he'll be into beer and late nights by then and it'll start all over again.

Both babies still wake at night and I'm sure they communicate in their own way, conspiring against Benjamin and me to ensure we don't have time to get intimate. Benjamin's complaining he's not getting enough greens.

I'm becoming clumsy, which I can only put down to the lack of sleep and darkness. I seem to knock into hidden objects that only appear on my route to the babies' rooms. Last night I walked straight into the cupboard door Benjamin had left open to try not to wake me when he left for work at five-thirty in the morning. It's pointless because I'm usually up anyway, but I didn't have the heart to tell him. I think it's his way of showing he cares. They're not supposed to wake in the night for a feed now, they're over the six months' mark, but seeing neither Jessica nor Benjamin have read these expert baby books, I'm not surprised they aren't abiding by the rules. During the long nights I have begun to make silent pacts with God, praying that in exchange for a single full night's sleep I'll be a better Christian and I'll attend church more often. I'm not sure He's listening though. Although I was never musically orientated, something you said was a shame, I'm becoming quite good at making up my own lullabies. It's one way to pass the time in the darkness of their rooms during those lonely hours at night. I'm sure only a mother really knows just how lonely you can feel.

Here's my latest lullaby, tell me what you think.

'Hush little baby don't say a word, it's time to sleep, it's time to sleep.

The fairies wait to welcome you, the fairies wait in dreamland.

It's now time to rest your head; it's now time to go to bed.

Close your eyes close your eyes.

Night is nigh, the day has gone. Babies resting peacefully.

Go to sleep my little ones.

Mummy, Daddy love you Noo, Mummy Daddy love you Noo.'

I told you I'm losing my mind, do you believe me now?
Hugs and kisses
Emma-Beez

Chapter Fifteen

The e-mail arrived from Anthony in our legal department, along with the attachments I was waiting for. Great, I thought, now I can see what's really been going on. As I suspected Jenny and Allan had renegotiated the original contract terms she and I had agreed to before I went on maternity leave. Typical, I thought, all that dribble about 'I'll protect your position for you' etc...etc...What a whore, she sold herself to the highest bidder.

Jenny and Allan had renegotiated a year's contract instead of a six-month contract, with a clause to extend at the end of that period and at a higher fee than originally agreed. In fact the fee if annualised worked out to be far in excess of my fixed annual salary. The cheek of it! Had Allan thought I'd not return to work now that I was a mother of two babies? Or had Jenny been conspiring behind my back from day one, communicating falsely that I was vacillating about returning and hence my commitment was wavering? She had played the fox well and I had fallen for it hook, line and sinker.

I felt cheated, betrayed, angry and at best disappointed. I knew the company's policy towards women was flawed but I had hoped they would have recognised my contributions and my skills and behaved differently towards me than they had to my fellow colleagues in the past. How naïve of me. My anger mounting, my head spinning, I had to put a plan of action in place. I wasn't going to be treated like this and I certainly wasn't going to let them get away with it. But what to do?

I picked up the phone to call Caroline Kirkland, a friend of ours who worked at a top legal firm in the City, and who herself was on maternity leave.

"Hello, Caroline Kirkland speaking."

"Hi Caroline, Emma here."

"How are you and Benjamin, how are the twins?"

"Fine, just fine thanks. How's Jacqueline?" I asked.

Jacqueline was Caroline's three-month-old daughter.

"She's a dream child, I couldn't have asked for a more perfectly behaved baby." I hated her for saying that. My odds should have been greater with two of having at least one 'perfectly behaved baby' but alas I'd drawn the short straw I thought.

"Caroline, can you give me some advice about a situation I have with work about returning after my maternity leave?" I asked.

"Sure, just a minute while I put Jacqueline down." There was a pause and then Caroline continued.

"Tell me what's going on."

I gave Caroline the run down of my sob story and how I felt I had a case against the company.

"Emma, it sounds as if there could be a case for sexual discrimination and unlawful practice with regards the course of events with the contractor," Caroline said as I finished my story.

"What do you recommend I should do?"

"Well, there are a few things you can do. One is walk away of course, two is seek legal advice from one of the partners in my firm, I'll give you her contact details or three speak to your boss and come to some form of mutual arrangement."

"Which of these would you pursue if you were in my shoes?"

"The truth Emma, is that any legal action is both time consuming and costly. Costly in both financial terms as well as emotional. You could still find yourself in legal discussions after six months and it may take up to a year to conclude. You'll have to fork out the money upfront and if you win, and only if you win the case, will you be compensated." Caroline laid the facts out in front of me.

"So what would you do?" I repeated my question.

"If I were you, I'd try and come to some form of arrangement with your company."

"I see. Could you give me the telephone number of the partner you mentioned anyway?" I asked.

"Caroline gave me the telephone number and I thanked her and we set a date to get together.

I then opened a new file and began to type an e-mail to Jenny Green.

Hi Jenny,
Hope you're well. Haven't heard back. Please forward a copy of your current contract to me as discussed earlier.
Cheers,
Emma

Although Jenny had promised to get back to me she hadn't which wasn't surprising knowing what I knew. What did surprise me was how long she thought she could play delay tactics with me and for how long she'd thought I'd fall for it. She must of underestimated me and thought me a complete fool!

It wasn't until two days later that I received a reply from Jenny.

Hi there Emma,
I hope you're well; I've been away for a couple of days. With regard to my contract that I signed with Allan Crawford, Allan has strictly forbidden me to send any documentation to you, which is standard procedure but it puts me in a difficult situation – and of course, this is a private matter so it is best if I stay out of it.

Catch up soon

Jxxx

Like hell she'd been away and she absolutely was slap bang right in the middle of the matter. I'd introduced her to the company and she had legally agreed to step into my role for a fixed period of time while I was on maternity leave and in the interim she had wangled herself into a position of strength and hijacked my job right from under my nose!

She'd used me, taken what she'd wanted and spat me out. I wondered how many other people she'd done this to during her consulting career.

I was damned if I'd walk away.

"McHammer and Associates may I help you?" the voice asked.

"Yes, I'd like to speak to Penelope Byrd please," I said.

"One moment please."

"Penelope Byrd's assistant, may I help you?"

"Yes, I'd like to speak to Ms Byrd please."

"May I ask whose calling?" she asked.

"My name is Emma Hogan, Caroline Kirkland referred me. I believe Caroline already briefed Ms Byrd," I said.

"Oh yes. One moment while I put you through she's just stepped out of a meeting."

"Mrs Hogan, I've been expecting your call," she said.

"So you've spoken to Caroline. That's good. How much detail has she given you?" I asked.

"Not much, just the headlines. I'd suggest that we meet at our office and bring anything in the way of supportive documentation you have with you. My colleague will analyse all this for us if you decide to go the legal route," Penelope said.

We agreed on a day and time.

I felt relieved that I had decided to seek legal advice, that way at least I would know my rights, whether I decided to exercise them or not.

Next on my plan of action was to call Allan Crawford.

"Allan, Emma speaking."

"Oh, Emma, I was about to call you. I'm in London actually," he said. Why he gave himself away like that I won't really ever understand.

"I thought we were going to meet while you were here. Or that's what you said in your last e-mail," I said accusingly.

"Yes, that's why I was about to call you but meetings have been back to back," Allan said defensively.

"I called to follow up our last conversation. I haven't seen a job description for my new role or a revised contract. What's going on?" I got straight to the point.

"Stewart and I haven't been able to connect yet," Allan said, lying through his teeth I could tell. Stewart was the head of Innovation and the man I would be reporting in to.

"Look Allan, let's cut to the chase. I'm returning to work, which you've known about for three months now as well as the fact that it's my basic right to do so. By law, the company is obliged to find me a position of equivalent seniority and remuneration. Why am I being messed around Allan? What's the real story?" I said, without losing control but clearly indicating my irritation with the whole situation.

"Emma, the company has restructured again and we've retrenched a number of global positions and others we've eliminated. There's no immediate role at your level of seniority basically that I can place you into right now."

"Well, why didn't you think about the repercussions for me earlier and why haven't you been direct with me from the start?" I was really pissed off.

"Emma, what I can put on the table for you with a flexible working schedule, is an administrative position in Innovation." Allan ignored my outburst as so he should have. "Which doesn't fall under my responsibility but rather Stewart's."

"What are you telling me?" I asked him plain and simply.

"There's no real role for you any longer. Jenny's working for us still and the global functions have disintegrated. I would suggest you take voluntary redundancy," Allan said.

It then dawned on me that he never had any intention of me returning to work after pregnancy and childbirth and he hadn't budgeted for my position. Jenny Green had taken up the role I had been playing and had wormed her way into a position of power somehow. I daren't think how, but perhaps... After all she was an attractive divorced woman with nothing to lose.

Now that I thought about it, there were no married women with young children in senior positions within the firm. In fact there was only one woman at directorship level in Corporate Affairs and she was divorced with two older children and sleeping with the chairman.

"I've only given birth to twins Allan, I haven't given birth to my brain you know. I'll be in touch shortly," and with that I put the phone down.

Benjamin and I were going out for dinner, alone at last! Sally-Ann was baby-sitting and I felt like a teenager who'd just passed their driver's licence, free as a bird!

Over dinner I told Benjamin what had happened with work and that I was going to seek legal advice.

"Good riddance to bad company," Benjamin said when I had finished.

"I knew you'd say something like that. I'm disappointed though, surely my skills meant more to them."

"Emma, you were just another employee at the end of the day and everyone, as much as you don't like to hear it, is ultimately dispensable," Benjamin said.

"I can't get over Jenny's dishonesty," I continued.

"I'd asked you why she sent gifts for the birth of Jessica and William and why she sent you a present at Christmas. It all seemed too planned to be innocent. She always had an eye for your position from the day you hired her to consult for you and she knew you were going on maternity leave. She needed the work Emma and you were easy meat," he said.

"Besides Emma, you were being unrealistic thinking you could go back to work with the babies as sick as they were," he added.

"I'm gullible," I concluded.

"Yes, you're naïve Emma, but that's why I love you so much," he said as he lent over the table and kissed me.

"You flatter me, what's your angle?" I asked jokingly.

"Ich will mit Dir unter einer Decke schlüpfen." I had once taught Benjamin a few sentences in German and there were two he had never forgotten. This was one.

"You'd better give the babies a sedative so they don't disturb us!"

While I was preparing for my meeting with Penelope Byrd an e-mail arrived in my inbox from an old school friend of mine who lived in London, but whom I hadn't seen for at least a year. It read:

Hi Emma,

It's been an age since I last saw you and we're living on the same island – shocking! My mother and your mother have been talking… the usual blah, blah, blah I'm sure, but your mother mentioned your difficulties with falling pregnant and suggested to my mother that I ask you for advice.

Jeremy and I've tried and tried for two years now. I think we need some help. Can you council me? I'm an emotional wreck.

Lucy
PS Never thought I'd see the day, but Jem's sick to death of sex!!'

I laughed quietly to myself recalling those desperate days. How ironic, this is the circle of life. I wrote back:

Hi Lucy,

Glad you're alive and kicking, must get together soon. I'd be delighted to help, give me a call now if you wish or anytime after eight at night is good.

Just then the telephone rang, Lucy I thought.

"Hello, Emma Hogan."

"Emma, it's Lucy, how are you?"

"I'm well, the twins are hard work but gorgeous," I said purposefully, keeping the gory stuff at bay not to dampen her spirits about babies.

"I need some advice about fertility Emma," Lucy said.

"Sure what do you need to know?"

"Jeremy and I've been trying for over two years. Some months I don't fall pregnant and others when I do I miscarry at around six to eight weeks into the pregnancy. I'm not sure who to see here and how to go about it. Who helped you and Benjamin?"

"I saw a doctor at the University College Hospital, Phoebe put me in touch with her. She's great. Her name is Dr Collins and I'll give you her contact details," I said, remembering how I was feeling this time a year ago.

"Did it take long once you got help?" she asked.

"No, the second time round. At the time it seemed like eternity but looking back it only took three months in all," I said.

"Lucy?" I asked.

"Yes, Emma," she said.

"Life sometimes feels like a marathon against time, but it really needn't be taken at such a pace. Take time out, the pieces will fall into place. Just a thought to keep you in the present, 'cause I've been there when you're wishing for tomorrow, praying for the day to come when you'll be holding your baby in your arms. There's too much good stuff in between, don't miss out on it," I said.

"Let's set a date to get together?" Lucy said, which we did before ending the call.

Once we had finished I sent Lucy the contact details via e-mail and included a little saying by an anonymous poet.

Look to this day for it is life,
For yesterday is already a dream
And tomorrow is only a vision.
But today, well lived, makes every yesterday
A dream of happiness, and every tomorrow
A vision of hope.

I compiled a summary of the sequence of events for my meeting with Penelope Byrd and put together a file containing all the correspondence I thought would be appropriate and could help build my case. I felt a little like John Grisham. I arrived at McHammer and Associates offices in the city centre and was told to take the elevator to the fifth floor.

The offices weren't as intimidating as I had imagined they'd be, so I began to relax and feel a little more at ease.

"Mrs Hogan please follow me, Penelope will see you shortly," Penelope's assistant said as she showed me into one of the meeting rooms.

"Can I get you something to drink?" she asked.

"Yes, some water would be nice thanks," I said dying of thirst. I always found the city so polluted. When I blew my nose a wad of black dirt came out. I was glad I had done this before Penelope had walked in. I could only imagine what the pollution was doing to my lungs! I might as well take up smoking, I thought, just as Penelope and a colleague, obviously her junior, entered the room.

"Mrs Hogan, I'm Penelope Byrd and this is Sean who works with me," she said as I stood and shook her hand and then Sean's.

"Thank you for seeing me at such short notice," I said, aware that it was only because of Caroline that I had managed to get an appointment so soon.

"I'm a mother of two myself so I can empathise with your situation," Penelope said and then continued. "What can we do for you?"

I explained my situation to her and handed her the file I had prepared and the executive summary of events. She listened and not once did she ask questions, she then read the summary while Sean took the file. Only once she had digested its contents did she begin to speak.

"Mrs Hogan it sounds as if your company has conducted themselves erroneously. I think there may well be a case for sexual discrimination and seeing you were really forced into opting for voluntary redundancy, a case for unfair dismissal. What I would suggest as an immediate course of action is to sit tight until the end of this month when in effect the contractor, Jenny Green I think you said her name was, should have completed her contract period as agreed by you and her before your maternity leave. I would then find out if she continues to work for the company come October and, if so, we can then draft a letter to the company asking a few questions about the termination of your employment, the company's women to men ratio at a senior and board level and so on. We typically find a letter from a legal firm threatening litigation does the trick and companies usually choose to settle long before a court hearing," Penelope said.

"How long do I have to file a suit against them if I choose to do so?" I asked.

"Three months," Penelope replied.

"I'll ask Sean to go through the paperwork you brought along and he'll give me the highlights. You don't want me, at my charge out rate, to do this arduous exercise," she said.

"What is your charge out rate?" I asked nervously. I knew most lawyers charged an arm and a leg, one reason why their offices were always filled with Persian rugs and mahogany furniture.

"Mine is £280 per hour and Sean's is £175." Phew, that's a shit load of money.

"I must set your expectations straight upfront Mrs Hogan. These cases can take up to a year to conclude and there is no guarantee that you will win. They're often messy and personal. All our costs must be paid in increments as they are incurred and only if you win will you be in a position to negotiate compensation, which includes any financial outlay you've incurred directly relating to the development of your case," Penelope said.

As she spoke I got a glimpse of what the next year would be like if I pursued the issue: hours of discussion and telephone calls; loads of personal insults; days of wondering what and when; nights without sleep; issues raised which should have been long forgotten; costs going through the roof and a family in tatters. Not a pleasant picture.

"Thank you Penelope, I'll need to discuss this with my husband and get back to you. When would you need to know if I wish to proceed?"

"By October," she said.

"Right, I'm a little nervous about the costs and the emotional stress a case like mine might bring upon my family. Obviously my decision will not be entirely based on my opinion but that of my husband's and what's best for the family unit," I said, trying to leave myself an exit strategy should we decide not to go ahead.

"Believe me Mrs Hogan, I more than understand." Penelope said this in a way that made me think she'd been through something like this herself at some point in her career.

Funny though, Sean hadn't said a word the entire meeting, but yet I was sure I'd be billed for his time.

I broached the subject of legal action with Benjamin, probably the worst possibly timed conversation I could have initiated. He was in the middle of getting his things together for a golf game, the first in around nine months. I should have known he would not be enthusiastic about the subject.

"I need to get back to the legal firm about my decision," I said, as I passed him his newly cleaned golfing socks from the dryer.

"Oh, I thought you'd already made up your mind," Benjamin said disinterestedly.

"First, no I haven't made up my mind and second, it's not my decision it's our decision," I said confrontationally.

"You know my views then don't you?" he said and turned away to focus on closing his kit bag.

"Can you just give me five minutes please, this is important?" I said firmly.

"Emma, why can't you just close that chapter and move on? What would you prove by engaging in legal action? It will only bring stress and unhappiness to our lives and it will affect not only you but me and both Jessica and William," he said adamantly.

"Then why did you entertain the idea in the first place?" I was confused. He had supported my actions and now all of a sudden he was making out as if he was against this from the start.

"I didn't really, you just don't give a man a chance to say no. I thought by letting you investigate your options you'd realise there was only one real one. That is to walk away."

"My pride is at stake," I protested.

"Emma, don't kid yourself, any legal battle strips you of your pride," Benjamin said, having been a witness in a legal suit three years prior.

So that was it then, I would drop any idea of legal action in the interests of my family and walk away.

"Emma, have you started packing?" Mum asked, her voice overflowing with pent up anticipation.

"Are you mad, we only leave in two weeks' time. I'll get around to it the day before I'm sure. Sally-Ann's going to pack the babies' suitcases for me and their food for the plane," I said.

My mother, the perfectionist, always packed well in advance of her journey and had her clothes laid out on the spare room bed weeks in advance, just to make sure everything was colour coded. I was also full of anticipation, at the prospect of course of seeing my parents and the rest of the family again with the twins, but also because I had an expectation that our trip to South Africa would prove to be a turning point in William's little life.

"I've arranged everything Emma. The nursery looks stunning. I've loaned car seats and travel cots and I've bought highchairs. Ed Shoshone has kindly lent us his Pajero for a month for you to use. Your father's put up the pool net and the playroom for them."

"Mum slow down you lost me at Pajero. But everything sounds terrific," I said, my head dizzy with the thought of the amount of preparation and stress going on at home right then, all for our visit over Christmas.

PART THREE

Chapter Sixteen

Dear Viv,

As you can well imagine it's been pandemonium for the past three days in preparation for the flight to SA. Way too much luggage and not enough room, thank goodness I'm not breast-feeding, the pump would have had to fit in my handbag! The flight started off perfectly. Jessica and William both fell asleep after taking a full feed and guess what? No vomiting. I didn't need the extra clothing. Then after two hours all hell broke loose and both babies didn't sleep a wink for the remaining nine hours, they screamed blue murder. At one point the situation became so untenable that one of the passengers at the back of the plane came forward and offered to relieve Benjamin or me, they felt so sorry for us.

It was such a relief to eventually touch down on terra firma and see Mum and Dad. I used to silently pray I wouldn't be sitting near a family with babies when they boarded a plane, now the shoe's on my foot, I feel guilty for ever having such selfish thoughts and being so heartless. Putting it into perspective – when you've survived a whole ten months without sleep, what's one night on an aeroplane? I am silently hoping that this trip will prove to be a turning point for William and his vomiting will cease. We're going to the beach for ten days while we're out. I've had withdrawal symptoms since we moved to the UK... the thought of sifting white, soft sand through my fingers and the rhythmic breaking of waves on the shoreline just turns me to jelly. Mum's in her element with all three of her pups around her for Christmas. Contrary to Mum's advice, I've decided against hiring a nanny while in SA. I think that I need to be able to cope on my own at some point. What better time to try than when I'm with family with a support structure around me? I'll probably regret this no doubt.

All my love
Emma-Beez

A few days passed. William's reflux got worse again and I became distressed. It was as if the medical world was conspiring against me.

Darling Viv,

Well I spoke too soon in my last letter to you. William started vomiting all over again and this time it's worse. He vomited on Mum three nights ago, which put Mum into a complete spin and messed up her newly done hairdo. She made me call a paediatrician the very next day, Dr Reighgate, we saw him today in fact. I told Mum that this is normal behaviour for William – same shit different day basically. Bottom line, I'm fed up with the medical profession; they just don't seem to get it Viv. William has a very severe problem, if indeed it is reflux as they say it is, then he's one of those few who, I think, needs an operation. He vomits in the middle of feeding and up to three hours after a feed just when you think it's safe. I am worried that if we leave it any longer it's going to affect other areas of his body like his lungs, chest, oesophagus and ears. As it is anyway, he's not putting on weight and he's what they call 'failing to thrive'. Dr Reighgate has prescribed an anti-acid medication and a food thickener. Yes, I know what you're going to say. 'But he's already been through all of this and it hasn't worked.' Well, you're right, dead right. The doctors just don't seem to believe me; they must think I'm neurotic. They're right of course about the neurotic bit, except that I'm becoming neurotic about them, not William's condition. I've agreed to go away to the coast and when we get back to see how he is. If it's no better by then, then I'm putting my foot down. So if you hear the earth tremor don't panic it's just me on the rampage.

I think, no in fact I know, the rest of the family particularly Chris, are sick to death of hearing about the problems we're having with William. I've probably put him and Fay off having children forever!

I'll keep you posted.
Lots of hugs and kisses
Emma-Beez

"Mum, could you ask Tony to ring Dr Quinn and see if he'll see William and me as soon as possible?" I had called Mum from the car on the way back from the coast. William had just vomited all over his car seat, just missing Jessica by an inch or two.

Tony, a great friend of ours, and a surgeon himself, knew Dr Quinn, one of the top paediatric surgeons. If any one could get us an appointment with him, it would be Tony.

"Why darling?"

"I'm fed up, William's no better, so much for this new anti-acid, he just vomits it up along with everything he eats or drinks. He is totally put off by any form of lumps in his solid food. If he tastes a lump he just vomits his food back up. I'm certain that this is also linked to his reflux."

"I'll see what I can do darling. I'm so sorry for you, for William." she said sympathetically.

"I know. He's tried for too long now, it's getting no better and it's been over ten months now."

"How far are you from home?" she asked.

"Benjamin how much longer have we got do you think?" I had no idea for how long we had been travelling, all I knew was I felt nauseous from the smell of sick.

"Emma, tell her we'll be home in around two hours if William doesn't get sick again," Benjamin said.

I relayed the message to Mum and prayed William would sleep for the remainder of the journey. Jessica was wide-awake, I'm sure the smell was also getting to her.

Mum had managed to contact Tony, and he in turn, had arranged for Dr Quinn to see William and me the Saturday after we arrived back from the coast. I hoped that Dr Quinn was going to be our knight in shining armour. I couldn't bear the thought of taking William back to the UK in his current condition. Benjamin had had to travel back to the UK for his work so I was left to deal with William.

"Dr Quinn, thank you for seeing us at such short notice," I said, as Mum and I greeted him outside the paediatric ward.

"No problem, come this way. This must be William?" Dr Quinn's focus was immediately directed on William.

We followed him into the ward and into a private consultation room at the end of the passageway.

"Now, what's William's history?" Dr Quinn was a man of few words.

I ran through William's history from birth until then and could not help but weep as I recalled every moment of his little life so far.

"He's a fighter then isn't he?" he said as he stroked William's head.

"What about his sister?" I suddenly felt guilty about the attention I had given William and the expectation I had that Jessica would just get on with things.

"I think we need to go in and see what's going on," Dr Quinn said without a moment's hesitation.

"What do you mean by go in and how soon can you do this?" bowled over that I had finally found a doctor who was prepared to investigate the problem.

"We will need to do a gastroscopy. This we do by putting a tube into William's mouth, down his oesophagus, his duodenum and into his stomach. We'll then be able to see if there are any ulcerations and the extent of these," Dr Quinn explained.

"And what if it's severe?"

"Then, if you permit, we'll perform a Nissan Fundiplication," Dr Quinn said, and then left the sentence hanging as if I had to guess how this would be performed.

"How is this procedure done?" I pressed on.

"In crude terms, we will twist part of his stomach around the oesophagus to act as the sphincter and prevent food and liquid from coming back up."

"What are the side effects?" I asked knowing most surgical procedures had some side effects.

"Very few and relative to what William's been through and the damage to other areas of the body, a severe and prolonged case of reflux can cause, I'd say minimal," Dr Quinn said, not answering the question directly.

"Just as a matter of interest what are these?"

"Some patients find it difficult to pass wind and patients are no longer able to vomit after the operation is performed."

"That'll penalise him at university," I said, thinking of all the drinking that usually goes on with boys in their early twenties.

"We only perform the procedure for a few set reasons which include failure to thrive, William's problem, recurring chest infections, continual loss of teeth and a few others," Dr Quinn went on.

"How soon can you perform the operation?" I asked expecting at least a three-week wait, which would prolong our stay in South Africa.

"This coming week is unusual in that I have haven't any procedures lined up for Monday afternoon, so I can do William then."

It couldn't be that after so many months of waiting we would finally know for definite what was going on with William?

"Well, you have a decision to make," Mum said, having been quiet during most of the conversation.

On the way home my mother asked how I felt about what Dr Quinn had said.

"It is like a double edged sword isn't it?"

"Yes, you don't have much choice really."

"I've made up my mind but I need to talk to Benjamin as I said to Dr Quinn and then let him know." I was going to call Benjamin that evening to talk him through the procedure and the few alternatives we had.

Meanwhile I looked over my shoulder at William in the back seat, sound asleep, exhausted from the whole encounter. I thought how wonderful it would be for him, to enjoy eating and drinking like a normal child.

That evening I called Benjamin at home in the UK.

"Darling, I met with Dr Quinn today."

"How did it go, what did he say our options are?" he asked, almost hoping that we could avoid surgery.

"There aren't any really. Either we leave William to continue to suffer which may result in permanent damage to his lungs, his chest and his oesophagus because the reflux is so bad, or we allow Dr Quinn to operate," I said.

"Are there any side effects form the operations?" Benjamin, as an investment banker, knew how to take a calculated risk and what information you needed in order to do so.

"Not many, Dr Quinn mentioned the inability to vomit after the operation and the difficulty in passing wind." I told Benjamin exactly what Dr Quinn had told me.

"Do we have a choice Emma?" Benjamin asked rhetorically. "I think we have to go ahead. If William were thriving then I'd say wait but he's not and hasn't been for months now."

"How soon can you come out to South Africa again?" Weary now that I'd have to handle this on my own without him. There was never a doubt in my mind that if surgery was the route to go, I'd do it in South Africa where we as a family had contacts in the medical fraternity and where I could rely on the support of my family.

Darling Viv,

William had the operation!

I must admit that I've never felt as vulnerable before, as I did when 'the men in green' approached me to take William into theatre. As I handed over my little boy to the anaesthetist, knowing that he was going to go under the knife and I had absolutely no influence over the outcome, my heart sank and I felt a chill down my spine. I don't think I'll ever go for that boob job now! Elective surgery – no way! Benjamin will have to put up with boobs gravitating southwards, at least for a while.

As it turns out, to add insult to injury, William had an inguinal hernia as well. This explains his peculiar crawling technique – flat on his stomach like a leopard instead of on all fours and his consistent reluctance to sit in his highchair at mealtimes. Poor kid Viv, he's had such a rough start.

His reflux was so severe that Dr Quinn found ulcerations all the way down his oesophagus. All I could say when I saw Dr Quinn later that evening doing his usual ward rounds, was 'thank you for giving me my son'. Why in the world Dr Marlow in the UK hadn't done a gastroscopy I'll never know?

Although William is leaps and bounds better than he was before the operation, these things take time to heal. I think I had too high an expectation though that this procedure would bring a miracle to William's life and that he'd be cured overnight. But as we all know reality is reality and miracles don't happen overnight.

It might take a while for William to drink normally again. They call it gas bloat when they cannot pass wind easily and don't like to drink too much at one time. He looks a little like an old man with a potbelly after he's eaten or drunk his milk. I've nicknamed him 'Puffer'.

This wasn't to be the last operation unfortunately as I soon discovered.

In short William's been under anaesthetic three times since I last wrote to you. First the procedure, second the dilatation and third the grommets. Oh, don't let me forget, in between all of this, he contracted bronchitis in hospital and had to be nebulised with steroids. I even managed to stay three nights in hospital with him over the course of these three weeks – that was enough for me. You can imagine the size of a cot bed with both William and I squeezed in it together. I may have permanently rearranged my spine I think!

The first operation was in itself successful. The only hiccup was the opening was too narrow for William and he couldn't or rather wouldn't eat anything and only drank sips of water for two days until we re-hospitalised him and Dr Quinn widened it slightly. He did this by putting a balloon like structure down his oesophagus to stretch the opening, but not too wide for fear of recreating the initial problem.

While he was in hospital for the second time he contracted bronchitis from another little boy.

It was just as well he contracted it because this led us to investigate his ears, which were full of fluid. He had what they call 'glue ear'.

I think all of this is interrelated. The vomit didn't just go up the oesophagus into his mouth and onto my newly laid carpets, but also up into his Eustachian tubes causing this build up of fluid behind the ear drum.

Now the grommets are in William has no excuse for not listening to me when I say 'no' to something!

One of the hardest aspects of this whole ordeal has been coping with the guilt I feel about neglecting Jessica, who has been so brave and well behaved as if she really understands what's going on. I've spent very little time with her over the past three weeks and yet she still holds out her arms to me when I get home from the hospital and just rests her head against my shoulder.

Benjamin has been keeping the airlines in business. He's been to and fro three times now to fetch his family but each *time William has either had to go back into hospital for another procedure or has been recovering from the last one. I am hoping that after the grommets he'll now be ready to fly home.*

I do sometimes secretly wish that it was me on that plane and not Benjamin. Oh for some time alone away from the constant worry!

If all goes well, the babies will be christened on Sunday week, thought I may as well have them christened here before we return to the UK.

And if things do go according to plan finally, we'll be on a plane back home, to the UK, on the Thursday following.

If I had of known our three week holiday in South Africa was going to turn out to be three months I would have packed fewer clothes, brought an extra suitcase and gone shopping while I was here! Retail therapy always works wonders, you should know, you were a fashion icon back in your heyday.

Viv, must dash the phone is ringing.

Lots of hugs and kisses

Emma-Beez

As I sealed Viv's letter and put it away I reached for my mobile phone to answer it.

"Emma, it's Allan Crawford." I nearly fell off my chair. My mind raced as I wondered why would he be calling me all these months after my departure?

"I'm a little taken aback, it's been months Allan. Why are you calling?" I asked now a little indignant, yet curious.

"I'm in London and decided to call to find out how you are doing, how the twins are and what you're up to?" Allan said sheepishly. "We do miss you at work."

How odd things are and how fickle life can sometimes be? Did he feel guilty for treating me the way he did, the way the company did?

"How do you think I'm doing Allan, after the way my maternity leave and return to work was handled?" It suddenly dawned on me that the three months had come and gone since my departure. Three months was the legal time frame in which I had to file a legal suit against them. Thereafter I couldn't touch them. They were now safe from any legal threat so Allan had nothing to lose by calling me and appeasing his guilt. That explained the deathly silence.

"Are you working again?"

"No. I'm writing a book and have decided to take some time off. It's hard to find work as a new mum with young twins." I didn't want to tell him too much about my home and work life. After all, he'd been responsible, even if he was acting as the messenger, for turning the latter upside down and bringing it to a grinding halt for a while.

"Well, I am in London for two days and thought it would be good to know how you are doing," Allan said, now aware I was not interested in continuing a long conversation with him. I have learnt though never to burn your bridges, so I didn't want to leave the conversation having been abrupt and rude.

"Thanks for calling Allan, I appreciate the interest. Perhaps one day you'll see my book in a bookstore and pick up a copy to read. Have a good trip and safe flight home." With that we ended the call.

I thought about the conversation and wondered if I should write a letter to Allan and let him know how I really felt about how he handled the situation or if I should even waste my time doing so. What would a personal letter like that accomplish anyway, other than soothe my soul?

I began to write that letter to Allan when I suddenly stopped. No matter how hard I tried, the words that came across were full of self-pity. I didn't want Allan or the company's pity, so I decided to close that chapter of my life and to make peace with it. That way I would be free to move on to a new one, leaving the baggage behind me.

Dear Viv,

This will be my last letter to you.

The twins are now a year old. When I say this I can't quite believe it myself! We had a very smooth flight back from South Africa. Jessica and William slept for nine hours, waking only twice asking for milk. Benjamin and I slept crouched up on the foot stools at the top of the business class sleeper beds, while the twins lay sound asleep on our seats stretched out like a pair of lizards baking in the midday sun. We didn't care so long as they were quiet and asleep. I think life with William will be a little easier now after his operations, at least my laundry bills won't be as high. My carpets can be cleaned now and I can throw away the latex gloves. Small mercies I suppose.

I've missed you this year and found it hard not to be able to share these times with you in person. We made a good team you and I when I was growing up didn't we?

My last wish is that you may rest in peace knowing that we're all going to be fine and are out of the woods now. I may always wonder what life would have been like with full term babies one at a time, but I'm at peace with what has happened and know that I was meant to have two at one time and have them early. It's taught me more than I care to relay.

I can now say goodbye to you, something I never did in person before you slipped away to join Bobby all those months ago. Circumstances never permitted me to and I apologise for not being at your funeral. I was there in spirit though.

I expect you and Bobby are doing everything you always dreamed of now. Have you been to India yet and have you bought that Thai silk ball gown?

Thank you for lending me your ears and for being my conduit enabling me to make peace with the way things turned out this past year. Although nothing was quite what I had imagined it would be, it has been all that I dreamed of.

The twins, my little miracles, were born the day you passed from this world to the next and I believe that they carry your fighting spirit within them.

Jessica and I are developing our relationship now William is better and thankfully I don't believe there're any permanent scars.

I can now turn my attention to Benjamin, my darling husband, and give him the care he so deserves after months and months of neglect and abuse.

Always and forever

Emma-Beez

I sealed Viv's letter and placed it along with all the others I'd written that past year to her in the top drawer of my desk. Just then, as I was getting up to attend to Jessica who seemed to have taken herself up the flight of stairs leading to the playroom with no way of turning around, the phone rang.

"Emma, it's Lucy. Thought you'd be pleased to know. The third cycle of IVF worked and I'm pregnant," she exclaimed with inexplicable joy.

"That's wonderful news how many weeks are you?" I asked delightedly.

"I'm ten weeks pregnant, but that's not all. I'm expecting twins." And as Lucy said those words I simply knowingly smiled.